YOU'VE COME A LONG WAY,

Maybe

YOU'VE COME A LONG WAY,

Maybe

SARAH, MICHELLE, HILLARY, AND THE SHAPING OF THE NEW AMERICAN WOMAN

LESLIE SANCHEZ

palgrave
macmillan

YOU'VE COME A LONG WAY, MAYBE
Copyright © Leslie Sanchez, 2009.
All rights reserved.

First published in 2009 by PALGRAVE MACMILLAN® in the United
States—a division of St. Martin's Press LLC, 175 Fifth Avenue, New
York, NY 10010.

Where this book is distributed in the UK, Europe and the rest of the
world, this is by Palgrave Macmillan, a division of Macmillan Publishers
Limited, registered in England, company number 785998, of Houndmills,
Basingstoke, Hampshire RG21 6XS.

Palgrave Macmillan is the global academic imprint of the above
companies and has companies and representatives throughout the world.

Palgrave® and Macmillan® are registered trademarks in the United
States, the United Kingdom, Europe and other countries.

ISBN 978-0-230-61816-9

Library of Congress Cataloging-in-Publication Data is available from the
Library of Congress.

A catalogue record of the book is available from the British Library.

Design by Newgen Imaging Systems, Ltd., Chennai, India

First edition: October 2009
10 9 8 7 6 5 4 3 2 1
Printed in the United States of America.

For mom, *with love*

"If my critics saw me walking over the Thames they would say it was because I couldn't swim."

—*Margaret Thatcher*

CONTENTS

ACKNOWLEDGMENTS

*W*RITING THIS BOOK would not have been possible without the contribution of so many friends and colleagues. As was the case with *Los Republicanos,* some gave an hour of their time; others, so much more, including Beth Sturgeon, Jose Nino, Suzanne Bellsnyder, Hilary Rosen, Thomas Riehle, Tammy Haddad, Jamal Simmons, Bobby Berk, Erwin Gomez, Victoria Vasques, Jamie Burke, Deborah Price, and Barbara McCaffrey.

I value and appreciate the insights of several people who were critical in shaping the content: V. Lance Tarrance, Jr., Peter Roff, and Jennifer M. McAndrew read countless drafts and sacrificed many days helping to condense my verbose prose; Carlos Hernandez and Crystal Feldman served as my talented research team; and John Paul Tran of John Paul Tran Photography contributed his time for the beautiful author's portrait. I also owe a particular debt to my dear friend and publicist, Mike Collins, who knows his business better than anyone in Washington.

I give special thanks to CNN's fine editors and producers, who made covering the 2008 election cycle an unforgettable experience.

Great thanks to the Twitterati, stars of new media, in this case, specifically Twitter, who were tremendously helpful in my ability to converge political analysis with the growing social media landscape: Leslie Ann Bradshaw and William Beutler of New Media Strategies; Culture Kitchen's Liza Sabater; Erin Kotecki Vest of Blogher.com; Kathleen McKinley, Teri Christoph, and Tabitha Hale of Smart Girl Politics; my favorite "pundit mom" Joanne

Bamberger; Bettina Inclan, Kathy Riordan, Matte Black, Liz Mair, and Torrey Charles Pocock of Torrey Charles and Willner Marketing.

To Airie Stuart, Jake Klisivitch, and Donna Cherry at Palgrave Macmillan, thank you for your tireless commitment to this project. You may be the most patient team in publishing!

I appreciate the prayers and inspiration from my dynamic sisterhood of girlfriends and countless Republican allies, who shared their time and insights in hopes of building a greater story.

Most importantly, to Wayne and my loving family—thank you for your tireless support, devotion, and patience!

Keep the faith always.

Leslie Sanchez
Washington, D.C.
July 2009

INTRODUCTION

YOU'VE COME A LONG WAY, MAYBE

*M*Y GRANDMOTHER GREW UP on the historic King Ranch in south Texas, where her father was an expert horseman who tamed the rugged terrain with other Mexican stockmen. They were known as *Los Kineños*—"King's people." On land plagued with drought and rattlesnakes, my grandmother cared for her father and her two brothers after her mother died during childbirth.

At the age of six, she forced her way into the one-room schoolhouse so that she could learn to read, just like her brothers did. At that time girls were not thought to need an education. She got married, gave birth to my mother and, in the 1940s, divorced her husband at a time when few people in her culture would even utter the word.

My mother was raised in a sparse, three-room house on the outskirts of Corpus Christi. She married my father, gave birth to my brother and me, and then, after my father left, got a divorce. She raised me in a one-bedroom apartment in Houston, where we experienced fear, loneliness, hunger, sadness, and, at times, defeat. Despite our very real poverty, our spirits thrived and, eventually, so did we.

So I believe in—and fight for—the equality of women. I do so, as we all do, based on my own personal experience and interpretation of "feminism." I may follow in the shadow, but not the specific footsteps, of Chicana feminists like Alma M. Garcia or organizations like the ill-fated Comisión Femenil Mexicana Nacional (National Mexican Women's Commission). I don't agree with the feminist agenda, at least as it is most commonly presented in the media. Yet, I am no less passionate about women's empowerment.

To me, the word "feminist" epitomizes the zealots of an earlier and more disruptive time. The kind of women who would look at you with smug satisfaction when they say things like Germaine Greer's comment: "Probably the only place where a man can feel really secure is in a maximum security prison, except for the imminent threat of release."

Those women, who were predominantly white, college educated, and, above all else, strident, were often rebelling against a world of middle- and upper-class privilege that I never knew. Hispanic women, while vocal—in the company of other Spanish-speaking women—tend to be more socially conservative and publicly demure. Who we really were was not reflected by the flamboyant Carmen Miranda or the skimpily dressed Spanish-language weather girl.

We had our own sisterhood called Las Comadres.[1] We were expressive in Spanish, silent in English. As a child growing up in south Texas, I watched the natural division of Hispanic men and women at Sunday backyard barbeques. Men drank beer. Women cooked and gossiped—about the men. Who needs a mommy's day out when you have an entire network of female relatives acutely versed in navigating a world of Mexican egos? We had no power, no external voice outside our network, but a consistent thread of compassion.

Outside the wood fences these women were mere shadows of their true selves. Less amplified, more restrictive—like wearing a shoe that's a little too tight. It was my perspective of the world until I moved to Washington, D.C.

The ideal I grew up admiring is an ideal that I think is shared among all women, not just among Hispanic women. It is how most women live their lives—guiding their families to keep them together, working within the shared values of their communities. We are respected leaders because we are proud, sometimes quiet, giants. We do what we do because we want to, not just because someone expects it of us. We've made a choice. And this is something we want our elected leaders to reflect as well. We want them to be—and we need them to be—like us because that way we know they share the values we hold most dear.

And it would be nice if, once in a while, these leaders were women too.

So far we haven't had much luck in that regard. In considering a subject like this one—the role of women in the leadership of our nation—it's pretty easy to get depressed. We represent more than half the voting-age population. We are a significant political force. We contribute our time and our money to candidates and causes we believe in. Yet when you consider that at present only six of the nation's fifty governors are women, or that of one hundred U.S. senators only seventeen are women, the situation seems grim. The United States lags behind many countries in the level of gender equity in elective office. Think of such iconic leaders as the United Kingdom's Margaret Thatcher, India's Indira Gandhi, and Israel's Golda Meir. Think of contemporary leaders like Angela Merkel, the German chancellor, or Yulia Tymoshenko. Never heard of Tymoshenko? Get to know her. She's twice been ranked by *Forbes* magazine as among the most powerful women in the world—in 2005, her ranking was third, just behind Condoleezza Rice—and she is currently the prime minister of Ukraine; many in her own country speak of her as a viable candidate in their next presidential election. And, in fact, while in the United States some people were energized by the fact that, should Hillary Clinton be elected to the presidency, her administration would be historic not only because she would be the first woman to hold that office, but also the first first lady to do so, Argentina is only the most recent among the countries that have beaten us to that punch. Cristina Kirchner, who served as her nation's first lady during her husband's administration, began her term as the country's first elected female president in October 2007, having beaten her nearest opponent by an amazing 22 percent.

But here in the United States our progress is lagging. "Well, wait a minute," you might say. "Not so fast. Wasn't it just during the 2008 presidential election that the American people witnessed the remarkable achievement of a woman as a major party contender for the presidential nomination in New York senator Hillary Rodham Clinton and the first woman on a Republican ticket in Alaska governor Sarah Palin?"

Yes. But it's also true that neither of their campaigns was ultimately successful. Still, you'd be right in that getting their names on the ballot wasn't the only barrier they broke—not even close.

First, CLINTON AND PALIN both proved that women can meet the all-important money test. It's a simple fact of political life: if you can't raise or don't have the money you need to run an effective campaign, you might as well stay home.

Hillary Clinton was the first woman to break this barrier, raising more than $100 million, which is a staggering amount for a primary campaign. Of course, she had been building a network for sixteen years, during the eight years her husband was president of the United States and during the eight years that George W. Bush occupied the White House. But, rather than see that as a caveat, it is actually the hallmark of a professional politician. Almost no one, Barack Obama being the exception that proves the rule, starts from nowhere and goes on to win the presidency—and he had to go outside the agreed-upon system to do it.

Sarah Palin's ability to raise money was immediate and game changing. According to NBC News, in just one eleven-*hour* period—

between 1 p.m. and midnight on the day Palin's vice-presidential candidacy was announced—the McCain campaign raised about $4.5 million.[2] Once the general election got under way, Palin turned her attention to raising money for the Republican National Committee and congressional candidates around the country. And though her ticket, as well as many other Republican candidates, lost that election, her personal success at raising funds continued.

Clinton and Palin proved it is no longer axiomatic that woman cannot raise the same kind of money as men seeking high political office. They can. But it was more than just their ability to raise money that made them so formidable; both Clinton and Palin energized the critical segments of the electorate and drew thousands to their rallies.

For all the missteps that followed, Palin's convention speech—her introduction to the nation—was a clear win for Palin personally and for the Republicans as a party. It generated huge television ratings and electrified the party, especially its conservative base, and gave McCain just about the only bounce he received during the entire fall campaign. The size of some of Palin's rallies rivaled Obama's in key battleground states like Florida and Virginia and it was clear to just about everyone that McCain picked her to win the election, not just to make a point, as was the case in 1984 when former vice president Walter Mondale chose New York congresswoman Geraldine Ferraro as his running mate.

Hillary Clinton competed in every Democratic primary and received on the order of 18 million votes before she conceded defeat to Barack Obama. She demonstrated genuine national appeal, among men and women, winning primaries in traditionally liberal states like California and Massachusetts and in traditional swing states like Ohio and Pennsylvania.

Standing on the shoulders of Geraldine Ferraro, Clinton and Palin achieved something in a way that no other American woman on the *national* political stage had before them.

But, for all these positives—and they are significant—we also witnessed a backlash against Clinton and Palin that won't soon be forgotten by American voters, especially women. Perhaps no other figures in recent political history have caused so much public and private hand-wringing and unleashed so much passion and vitriol as Hillary Clinton and Sarah Palin.

Clinton and Palin were very different women from very different backgrounds, but their commonality was the way they were treated by their colleagues, the media, and potential voters. Remember back in 2007, when one of Clinton's clothing choices seemed to rivet our attention? *Washington Post* staff writer Robin Givhan put it this way in a July 20 article for that newspaper:

> There was cleavage on display Wednesday afternoon on C-SPAN2. It belonged to Senator Hillary Clinton. She was talking on the Senate floor about the burdensome cost of higher education. She was wearing a rose-colored blazer over a black top. The neckline sat low on her chest and had a subtle V-shape. The cleavage registered after only a quick glance. No scrunch-faced scrutiny was necessary. There wasn't an unseemly amount of cleavage showing, but there it was. Undeniable.[3]

From the uproar over the astonishing fact that Hillary Clinton had cleavage to the obsession with Sarah Palin's wardrobe and her family, issues got buried, and sexism had nowhere to hide—and it could not be explained away in a partisan fashion. We were treated to cutting-edge punditry from folks like MSNBC's Chris Matthews, who summed up Senator Clinton's professional career by reminding us that "the reason she's a U.S. senator, the reason she's a candidate for President, the reason she may be a front runner, is that her husband messed around. That's how she got to be senator from New York. . . . She didn't win there on her merit. She won because everybody felt, 'My God, this woman stood up under humiliation,' right? That's what happened."[4]

In a few sentences Matthews dismissed all thought of Clinton's Yale Law School degree, her decades of legal experience, her work on the committee considering the impeachment of Richard Nixon, her appointment by Jimmy Carter in 1978 as the first woman to chair the Legal Services Corporation, and her record in the U.S.

Senate. She was reduced to a pitiable victim: the electorate was supposedly trying to compensate for a private betrayal by giving her a shot at the nation's highest public office. Does that come anywhere near sounding "right" to you?

For Palin it was, in many ways, even uglier. Unlike Clinton, who came to the election with two decades on the world stage already behind her, Palin was a veritable unknown. She had to introduce herself to the American public, but just as she was starting to do that, the media stepped in to explain to the American electorate who she *really* was. The worst of it was online, where the lack of standards and objectivity managed to eclipse even Chris Matthews's comments about Clinton. For example, AskMen.com posted this pressing question of the day: "Is Sarah Palin hot?"

> Since being revealed as John McCain's running mate in the 2008 presidential election, Sarah Palin has had the media buzzing about her back story: she's a long-time NRA member, she can fly planes, she was a star athlete and—of particular interest to men—she was a runner-up in the Miss Alaska pageant. And while her days competing in beauty pageants may be long behind her, Palin's current physical appearance has been lauded by many as one of the best, if not the finest, in public office. In fact, the possibility that Sarah Palin may become the next vice president has already inspired her internet admirers to label her a VPILF.[5]

I won't dignify that acronym further by explaining what it means. But AskMen's readers were quick to respond. Those who thought she was hot wanted to do things like "pound her snatch so hard it would hurt for days." Those who demurred? "Come on, Hillary is 60+ years old. That's not even fair." I always like a little ageism thrown in with my sexism, don't you? The country was in the middle of fighting two wars and an economic meltdown was beginning. This was the level of discourse that was going on? Didn't any of these guys want to hear what Sarah Palin had to *say?*

But let's not be sexist ourselves. It wasn't just men who "dissed" these two groundbreaking women candidates. In a now-infamous piece for the *Washington Post*, Charlotte Allen asked us to

[t]ake Hillary Rodham Clinton's campaign. By all measures, she has run one of the worst—and yes, stupidest—presidential races in recent history, marred by every stereotypical flaw of the female sex. As far as I'm concerned, she has proved that she can't debate—viz. her televised one-on-one against Obama last Tuesday, which consisted largely of complaining that she had to answer questions first and putting the audience to sleep with minutiae about her health coverage mandate. She has whined (via her aides) like the teacher's pet in grade school that the boys are ganging up on her when she's bested by male rivals. She has wept on the campaign trail, even though everyone knows that tears are the last refuge of losers. And she is tellingly dependent on her husband.[6]

Juxtapose this with Joy Behar's calling Palin "dumb," Sarah Silverman's calling her "gross," and Tina Fey . . . well, let's leave Tina Fey for a little later. The point is that it was women who were the most unkind to the two women candidates. Clinton and Palin both inspired great passion among segments of the electorate—and they both inspired something darker in the opposing camp. Clinton and Palin were running for the two highest offices in the land but, somehow, their candidacies turned us into mean girls.

Rosalind Wiseman, who wrote the book on which the movie *Mean Girls* (2004) was based, told me in April 2009, "Understand you don't have to be twelve to act like you're twelve. What it comes down to is intellectual vigor and engagement. It's about thoughtful processing. What gets in the way with us as women is we don't have a script. We haven't been told or taught how to speak to each other when we are in disagreement, and do it in a way where we don't take it personally."[7]

After the election a very different and terrifically underreported story started to emerge. A survey commissioned by the Lifetime Networks found that 65 percent of women—majorities in *every* demographic and political group—agreed "that male and female candidates are held to different standards on the campaign trail." In particular, they found that 64 percent of women "thought the coverage of Palin was more negative than that of other candidates running for office," with 79 percent saying "there was too much coverage of Sarah Palin's clothing" and 44 percent saying "there was an over-abundance of coverage of Hillary Clinton's wardrobe."[8]

The 2008 campaign featured the strong influence of women in the media—both from traditional outlets and the blogosphere. It certainly can be argued that CBS News anchor Katie Couric conducted the seminal interview of the campaign season. And, for perhaps the first time in American history we saw *female* television stars—most notably the aforementioned Tina Fey—shaping the public discourse throughout the campaign.

In some instances, prominent women in the media spoke out against sexist treatment they perceived Clinton and Palin to be receiving. This included Couric, ABC's Cokie Roberts, and CNN's Campbell Brown and Dana Bash, to name a few. Brown called the focus on Palin's clothes "an incredible double standard." Palin's $150,000 wardrobe, she said, was a "peripheral" issue and she challenged the media to "keep the focus on what really matters."[9] And Couric argued that "One of the great lessons of [Hillary Clinton's] campaign is the continued and accepted role of sexism in American life, particularly in the media . . ."[10]

On the blogs, women pulled no punches. When Elaine Lafferty, a Democrat, feminist, and former editor of *Ms.* magazine (who also happened to be a McCain-Palin supporter), strongly defended both Palin's intelligence and her right to run in a series of articles on The Daily Beast, she was skewered. One blogger on Jezebel.com posted an entry pithily titled, "Elaine Lafferty Is Stupid: As far as I'm concerned, former *Ms.* Editor Elaine Lafferty can go f**k herself."[11]

The 2008 campaign also saw social media networks explode in popularity, but only the Obama campaign harnessed its potential. With the exception of conservative young voters who became Texas congressman Ron Paul's social media army, most campaigners misread the role of new media. A quick review of Facebook reveals any number of groups revolving around the support—or vilification—of one candidate or another:

- "I have more Foreign Policy Experience than Sarah Palin," a group with over 200,000 members, and "1,000,000 Strong Against Sarah Palin," with nearly as many.
- "Women Against Sarah Palin"—not to be confused with "*Intelligent* Women Against Sarah Palin."
- Palin's own official page, with more than 500,000 registered supporters.
- "Stop Hillary Clinton: One Million Strong AGAINST Hillary," with over 800,000 members.

These informal networks, both virtual and in campaign head-quarters across the nation, sprung up to rise to the defense of "their" candidate. Tight-knit and highly partisan cliques such as the "sisterhood of the traveling pantsuits," as Hillary Clinton would later dub her faithful during her address to the Democratic National Convention, abounded.

But the makeup of these groups is also a compelling question. What did the Clinton "sisterhood" actually look like? Certainly there was a profound age gap among American women voters. Many young women argued for a new feminism—or even a post-feminist political environment—that both Hillary Clinton and Sarah Palin had trouble tapping into. How to appeal to those voters, I believe, is the main challenge facing the next female to throw her hat into the presidential ring.

*B*UT THE 2008 CAMPAIGN wasn't just about Sarah Palin and Hillary Clinton. There were other modern working women who played important roles, especially Michelle Obama and Cindy Mc-Cain. And so, to really understand the impact women had on the campaign, we have to look at them as well.

Michelle Obama and Cindy McCain, like other prospective first ladies before them, both mattered deeply to their respective campaigns—and not only because one of them would soon become one of the most visible if not powerful woman in America.

Mrs. Obama and Mrs. McCain mattered in ways that helped determine the outcome of the election. Whether or not we might think it's germane, a candidate's spouse (and, to a lesser extent, his or her family) is part of the package that is examined by voters. In August 2008, Gallup asked respondents, "When you are considering which presidential candidate to vote for, how important is the candidate's spouse in your decision?" Overall, 52 percent of people answered either "very important" or "somewhat important," with Republicans "slightly more likely" to say the candidate's spouse matters than were Democrats.[12]

It's not unreasonable then to say that in 2008, American voters were, at least in part, making up their minds about John McCain and Barack Obama based on what they thought of their wives. Throughout the campaign, both Cindy McCain and Michelle Obama were about equally known and liked by the American public. According to Gallup, immediately after both conventions, 54 percent of those surveyed held a favorable view of Michelle Obama, while 30 percent held an unfavorable one. In that same survey period, 51 percent viewed Cindy McCain favorably, while 24 percent held an unfavorable view of her.[13]

Recognizing the popularity of the wives, and their possible positive influence, the campaigns sent Mrs. McCain and Mrs. Obama out to stump for their husbands—often in key battleground states. As the *New York Times* reported, "Mrs. Obama is being deployed where it matters most. Since Labor Day, she has spent three days campaigning in Florida and two days each in Indiana, Michigan, North Carolina, Ohio and Pennsylvania, as well as days in other swing states (sometimes two in a day)."[14] And wherever they went, they made news—and not always *good* news for the campaigns, as when Michelle Obama said that "for the first time in my adult life I am proud of my country because it feels like hope is finally making a comeback."[15]

Ultimately, Michelle Obama became the country's first lady. Like Sarah Palin, before the election Mrs. Obama had been an ordinary hardworking mom, albeit one who wasn't running for political office, so she was subjected to a great deal less press scrutiny than was Palin. Mrs. Obama had also made it clear during the election that, should her husband win office, she would not return to her $300,000-a-year job as a hospital administrator but would instead be the nation's "first mom."[16] After the election, of course, that's exactly what Mrs. Obama did and, I suspect, that has a great deal to do with the favorability numbers in the high 60 percent range that she now enjoys.

This raises another question I want to explore in this book: Had Mrs. Obama tried to insert herself into her husband's policy-making team—à la Hillary Clinton, another former high-powered lawyer circa 1992—would we like her as much as we do, or would she be liked as much as the polling data suggest she is? Or would her policy role have generated the same kinds of controversies that befell Clinton during her eight years as first lady? Is a powerful woman, which is clearly how Mrs. Obama wants to be seen, more palatable to us in a politically peripheral role like first lady than as president or vice president? Is a more politically ambitious woman, like Clinton or Palin, always going to have trouble winning our affections? If so, what does that forebode about the possibility for a female candidate the next time one is on a national ballot?

For all that, it was Barack Obama who reached female voters most effectively. As CNN senior political correspondent Candy Crowley told me, on the campaign trail she was struck by the extent to which "younger women felt it was a much bigger deal to vote for a black man" than for a woman; when it came to the women's movement, they "were unaware that the fight goes on."[17] But what fight was Crowley talking about? The one from the 1960s and early 1970s of which Clinton was a veteran? To young women who grew up unaware of the disadvantages their mothers and grandmothers lived through, the victories of those earlier generations seem ancient history: they don't find them relevant to their lives today. Would Palin's brand of female power—the very image of the Prairie Madonna, a baby on one hip and a rifle resting against the other—have been more appealing were it not for the hordes of reporters descending into her hometown with the express purpose of debunking the very image she was trying to convey?

As in previous elections, women voters were very important to the outcome of the election. The fact that women vote in overwhelming numbers couldn't have been news to either camp—in fact, Clinton's campaign was in large part based on the assumption that women would vote in record numbers for one of their own—so why was the presentation of the candidates to female voters handled so clumsily by both parties?

Though the announcement of Sarah Palin as John McCain's running mate initially resulted in a surge of support from women—white women, in particular—the subsequent rollout was botched and the bounce did not hold. In the end, women went for Obama-Biden in large numbers, reinforcing the traditional gender gap advantage in favor of the Democrats, while Obama and McCain essentially split the male vote. Overall, 56 percent of women voted for Obama-Biden versus 43 percent for McCain-Palin. And Obama's percentage of women was considerably higher than Senator John F. Kerry's 51 percent in 2004. The gap was most staggering among unmarried women (single, separated, divorced, or widowed), who voted for Obama 70 percent to 29 percent; married women voted for McCain by a much slimmer margin—50 percent to 47 percent.[18]

These results raise a couple of interesting questions. Is it possible that women could have both disapproved of Sarah Palin as a potential vice president and disapproved of the way she was treated by the press? And might these women have approved of a Vice President Palin had Palin herself—rather than a misguided McCain campaign or a roster of comedians—defined herself for the American people? I think the answer to both questions is a resounding "Yes."

Palin was certainly more like these women than any of the other three major party nominees—she was a woman. An extraordinary woman. Guiding her family to keep them together, operating within the values of her community, and demonstrating she is the very model of a modern working mom. What stood in the way of these women heartily embracing one of their own? It's true that people don't tend to base their vote for president—for or against—on the running mate, but you would think these numbers would have translated into some kind of stronger support for McCain if the mainstream media had not been so negative about Palin.

These are a few of the issues I want to take up in this book. What were the dynamics that kept Sarah Palin from the White House? And what lessons can the next female candidate for high office take away from Palin's experience in a national campaign?

So, what it will take for a woman to—at long last—make it to the Oval Office? It did not happen in 2008, though the door was certainly opened. What will it take to finally get through the door? Some, like Camille Paglia writing for Salon.com, have argued part of the reason we have not yet seen a woman president is directly related to the fact that the head of our government is also the head of our armed forces.

> In the U.S., the ultimate glass ceiling has been fiendishly compli-
> cated for women by the unique peculiarity that our president
> must also serve as commander in chief of the armed forces.
> Women have risen to the top in other countries by securing the
> leadership of their parties and then being routinely promoted to
> prime minister when that party won at the polls. But a woman
> candidate for president of the U.S. must show a potential capac-
> ity for military affairs and decision-making.[19]

But that notion was, at least partially, complicated in 2008. Hillary Clinton routinely led her opponents on questions of "experience" and whether she would be a good commander in chief. In fact, the very idea—which Clinton's campaign promulgated at every possible turn—that we must elect a president who is "ready on day one" appeared to be profoundly rejected by voters during both the Democratic primaries and the general election.

Clinton's campaign suffered in part because it wasn't in tune with what the American people wanted—and because, in spite of the obvious gender novelty, Clinton was perceived to be the ultimate Washington insider. "Change versus more of the same," anyone? Though McCain-Palin tried to push their theme of "reform" and "shaking up Washington"—including the first woman vice president, who would be decidedly different from all vice presidents before her—Republicans couldn't differentiate themselves from an unpopular set of policies associated with the then-incumbent administration. More business as usual, the voters concluded, and they were ready for something new.

Adapting your campaign to reflect what voters want—which would seem to be the obvious thing to do if you're trying to get the job of representing the voters—is only part of the puzzle. As I'll discuss throughout the book, other lessons from the 2008 campaign for future candidates—both women and men—are clear, but they are also complicated. There are, however, a few things we can say with confidence:

- Young voters and the idealism they represent are an important and growing piece of the electoral puzzle; ignoring them—or appearing to—is perilous. This is particularly true for young women voters, who cast their ballots in higher numbers than their male counterparts. Politically speaking, this is more of a problem for Republicans—as young people and particularly young women trend Democratic—though it is not an insurmountable one, in my view. Studies have shown that for young voters, the message is less important than is making a quality, in-person contact and engaging them in a meaningful way. What is it that young women want of the person who holds the presidency? This is going to be a key question that will determine the fate of future campaigns.
- Related to this, social media (blogs, Facebook, Twitter, and whatever is next) were a major part of the 2008 campaign

and will only grow in relative importance. More and more people are becoming involved in online communities—including those older than the eighteen to twenty-nine set. Tapping into this technology will become increasingly essential for defining a candidate and his or her policy positions in the current environment of instantaneous feedback and decision making. Palin was the most obvious loser in this regard in 2008.

- Ultimately, the hardest task for the candidates in the next presidential election, however, may well be how to win over women voters in the twenty-five to fifty age demographic—especially if that candidate is a woman. This is a diverse grouping of voters: stay-at-home mothers, working mothers, and young, single women focused solely on their careers at one end, and women who have had the experience of being one or all three of those things at some point in their lives at the other. Is there a woman who can bridge these experiences to appeal to a broad swath of all of these various groups without triggering the backlash that occurred with Clinton and Palin? Does she exist, that woman who is enough like all of us that she can keep us from turning into mean girls?

On the positive side, though the 2008 election contained its share of brutal treatment toward the women candidates, and though neither Clinton nor Palin was victorious, the American people remain open to the possibility of a woman president. An ABC News–*Washington Post* poll in May 2008 found that 84 percent of people said that they themselves would be "entirely" (62 percent sixty) or "somewhat" (22 percent) comfortable with "a woman president of the United States."[20] That's a clear majority—if one party or the other can nurture in the next four to eight years the woman who has the ability to demonstrate the wider appeal that will be necessary.

Moreover, in spite of the polarizing effect of the recent candidates, the experience of Clinton's and Palin's runs has had an encouraging effect for women. By "a margin of more than twelve-to-one, women declared the 2008 election cycle a 'step forward' . . . toward electing the first female President of the United States."[21] And this was particularly true among girls. A survey conducted after the election by the Girl Scout Research Initiative of thirteen- to seventeen-year-olds found that "71 percent of girls believe it is likely that a woman will be elected as president in the United States within the next ten years; 22 percent believe it will 'definitely' happen."[22] My question in this book is, How do we make it happen?

It's important to recognize—though race is not the subject of this book—that the election of the first black president of the United States is not only a momentous and historic achievement for our country, it is a proud one for the vast majority of Americans as well. After the election, fully two-thirds of those surveyed by Gallup described their reaction to Barack Obama's election as "proud" (67 percent) and "optimistic" (another 67 percent). Seventy percent thought that race relations would improve (either "a lot" or "a little") as a result of his election.[23] Fifty-nine percent of girls and 52 percent of boys reported that the election had a positive impact on their confidence in being able to achieve their goals in the future—and 51 percent of girls and 45 percent of boys said it "positively impacted their confidence in being able to change things in this country."[24]

It is not entirely clear what this means for women—though the election of a woman to the highest office in the land would certainly be yet another equally momentous and historic election outcome. The 2008 election was an important step in that direction: it has changed the equation about who can lead the United States of America. But now, let's move on and talk about the campaigns we have recently witnessed and the lessons the next candidate for president—male or female—can take from them. Let's start to focus on the task of defining a new model for "feminism" that might just give a female candidate the leading edge at last.

1

THE SISTERHOOD
OF THE TRAVELING
PANTSUITS

*S*ENATOR HILLARY RODHAM CLINTON came into the 2008 presidential campaign as the presumptive Democratic nominee. Indeed, the word most often used to describe her candidacy was "inevitable." It was hers to lose—and she did. The question is, why? And, for the purposes of this book, what can other candidates—especially women—learn from her defeat?

We have much to learn from Clinton, and I'm not the only one who thinks so. As Hilary Rosen, an editor-at-large for the Huffington Post and a frequent CNN political contributor, told me,

> I think the evolution of Hillary as a candidate is very instructive and analogous to the evolution of women generally as candidates. When they started the presidential campaign, they thought that Hillary was going to have to establish her credibility as commander in chief—that it would really be her biggest and most consistent hurdle. What they came to understand was that through the course of her normal work Hillary had already established her credentials from a policy perspective. So what people wanted to understand was what the advantages to being a female candidate were—[does she] understand what it feels like for the waitress who is supporting two kids and a mother at

home and who has a job that isn't secure with no health care. People were looking to Hillary to be a candidate for women at the outset, when she really wasn't. She was a candidate for women in name only; not in demeanor and policy.[1]

But what does it mean to be a candidate for women in terms of *demeanor and policy?*

I too learned a great deal from Clinton. I was impressed by her as a savvy political candidate. We can argue over the packaging, but I think she succeeded, as far as the Democrats were concerned, in demonstrating that she was a strong contender who clearly articulated policies about which she was passionate. I didn't agree with most of her positions, and I confess that I was a little chilled by her unemotional delivery.

As I watched her grow as a candidate my appreciation for what she had managed to accomplish increased. In the end, however, it wasn't enough. Despite her advantages real and perceived, the American people rejected her. Her defeat was a stunning collapse. But why? Why was she unable to turn all of her advantages into a nomination for president? Part of the reason was a misguided assumption about how women—women of *all* ages—would vote.

In June 2007, an ABC News–*Washington Post* poll had Senator Clinton leading Senator Obama by fifteen points. The poll also showed that her margin was almost entirely attributable to her sizeable lead among women.[2] She was leading by about two-to-one among Democratic women. Her base of support was overwhelmingly female and, it now seems, Clinton and her campaign staff took it for granted that almost all women voters would just naturally vote for a woman. According to CNN senior political correspondent Candy Crowley, who covered Clinton's campaign, "it was part of their operating plan. Women were going to vote for Hillary."[3] Could it really have been that cut and dried?

Taking the women's vote for granted was the foundation of Clinton's strategy from the beginning. As reported by Joshua

Green of the *Atlantic,* a March 19, 2007, memo from Clinton's chief strategist Mark Penn said in part: "Our winning strategy builds from a base of women, builds on top of that a lower and middle class constituency, and seeks to minimize [Obama's] advantages with the high class Democrats."

The early data confirmed the apparent wisdom of this strategy. The very poll showing Clinton leading overwhelmingly among women also found that "Clinton is drawing especially strong support from lower-income, lesser-educated women—voters her campaign strategists describe as 'women with needs.' Obama, by contrast, is faring better among highly educated women, who his campaign says are interested in elevating the political discourse."[4]

Still, her lead among likely Democratic primary voters held strong as 2007 went on. A *USA Today*–Gallup poll conducted in September 2007 put her twenty points ahead of Obama. She led in *all* regions of the country and was favored by a whopping twenty-three points among women (48 percent to Obama's 25 percent).[5]

When you consider all of the factors aligning in Clinton's favor—the pathbreaking nature of her campaign to become the first woman president of the United States, her strong early lead, the data attributing this lead in large measure to support from women voters, *and* the fact that women make up a majority of Democratic primary voters—her failure to capture the nomination is that much more stunning. And, apparently, it was pretty shocking to her campaign as well.

In Hilary Rosen's analysis, Clinton's campaign "assumed that while Hillary was convincing the men and political elite in this country that she had the commander in chief chops, she could organize a women's camp almost as an adjunct, without having to publicly appeal to women on any level. . . . But what she wasn't giving them was a spiritual message . . ."[6]

And that decision, to run as a potential commander in chief (while it might have seemed intuitive, considering that the country was fighting unpopular wars on two fronts), came back to bite her. Absolutely everything changed on January 3, 2008, when Senator Barack Obama won the Democratic caucuses in Iowa with 38 percent of the vote in what caucus goers in this early state made into a three-way race—former senator John Edwards finished second (with 30 percent). Hillary Clinton's third-place, 29-percent finish proved disastrous to her presidential ambitions.

Perhaps most striking is that she lost among women in Iowa. According to CNN entrance polling data, 57 percent of Iowa Democratic caucus goers were women and the majority of them went for Obama. Politico.com's entrance polling found that Clinton won only 30 percent of women to Obama's 33 percent. Clinton lost among other groups as well, of course—men and first-time caucus goers. But most ominous was how her loss among women voters broke down: while she maintained a slight edge among married and older women, Clinton overwhelmingly lost *young* women. Obama did not just win the youngest voters—though he did so convincingly with 57 percent of their vote—entrance polling had him up among thirty- to forty-four-year-olds as well.[7] Was Obama delivering the "spiritual message" Rosen feels was lacking in Clinton's campaign? Was Obama getting more traction with young voters because, as Dan Gerstein wrote in *Forbes* magazine in April 2009, it was "a time when young voters in particular are feeling a much more acute sense of insecurity . . . 52 percent of respondents reported they were one paycheck away from having to borrow money from their parents or going into credit card debt."[8] Was Obama making his case for his economic plan with more boldness than Clinton at a time when the economy was on everyone's list of top ten worries?[9] And—this is a critical question—if Clinton had recognized and/or acted on what the women in Iowa seemed to be telling her in January, if she had reinvented her campaign at that point, would it have made a difference to the outcome, or was it already too late?

If Clinton had tried to revamp her message, what impact could be expected from the media's response?

It is in the experience of Rachel Sklar, a former political editor at the Huffington Post and a subsequent contributor to The Daily

Beast, that the key problem of Clinton's campaign may be revealed. Sklar is a Canadian, and, as she puts it, she came to this country with "no Clinton baggage." But "what veteran reporters tell me is she's pissed a lot of people off. . . . It wasn't popular to be a fan of Hillary Clinton, especially among the press."[10]

Sklar went on to say, in an interview with National Public Radio's Bob Garfield, concerning the bad blood between the mainstream media and the Clintons: "there's no question that there is history here . . . which is basically the default assumption of the media that anytime a Clinton does something, it's usually with ill intent."[11]

It is telling that, in order to counteract negative perceptions of Clinton during her run for the Senate in 2000, she went on a "Listening Tour," ostensibly to hear the concerns of the people in New York. In reality, it was an attempt to soften Clinton's image, to make her "likable."

While this "Listening Tour" apparently made some impact on the citizens—as evidenced by the fact that the people of New York did end up electing her to represent them by a margin of 55 percent to her opponent's 43 percent—the press was not nearly as swayed by the gesture. And this was a phenomenon that continued on into her run for president.

In fact, even the very liberal media, as represented by the talking heads on what we now understand to be the very Obama-friendly MSNBC, were not disposed to like her very much. Keith Olbermann even famously suggested that, to convince Clinton to concede, the Democrats might need to find "somebody who can take her into a room and only he comes out."

Would the press have responded favorably even if Clinton had tried to change her tack in the course of the campaign and started to deliver that softer spiritual message that women were clearly waiting so eagerly to hear? Given the vitriol from Olbermann, I have my doubts.

Even more to the point of this book, I have to ask myself if I remember a male politician who was required to go on any sort of "likability tour" to prove that, in addition to being a tough candidate for commander in chief, he could also be warm and fuzzy. John F. Kerry, who is known for his aloof Ivy League distance, never went on a likability crusade. For better or for worse, the Democrats had selected him as their candidate, and he was allowed to present himself as who he was. Though it did turn out to be for worse—after all, he lost the 2004 election to George Bush—there was never a hint that he should try to change who he was in order to gain the favor of the voters. Even John McCain, whose physical limitations translated to gruffness or crankiness for some voters, was not asked to transform himself into a warm and fuzzy candidate.

As Patti Solis Doyle, Clinton's former campaign manager told me, a number of the male members of Clinton's coterie advised that they "very much . . . wanted to see the funny Hillary, the Hillary we know and like. . . . Their point was, everyone knows she's tough, strong and qualified. Where's the Hillary we all know and like. . . . We proactively stayed away from branding her the woman candidate. In retrospect, that could have been a mistake."[12] So it's significant to note that it was only the woman candidate whose loss is, at least partially, blamed on the fact that the people just didn't like her enough.

In Iowa, Clinton did not capture the support of young women voters. This age gap, particularly among women, would become a vexing problem for Clinton. In many ways, she had set up her campaign to win a gender war, but she ended up losing a generational one. And it raises questions that are still unanswered: Why did young women feel more of a draw to Obama than to Clinton? Was it purely his message? His issue positions, which were not remarkably different from Clinton's own? Why didn't these young women "take up the fight" that their mothers and grandmothers had started? Why didn't they see themselves as part of it?

As Doyle admits, the Clinton campaign didn't reach out to these younger voters. "Anybody who knows anything about Iowa always says they're going to bring out the young voters. But they are never going to come out, especially during the holidays—school vacations, they're just not going to come out. David Yepson [the chief political correspondent for the *Des Moines Register*] said it. We bought that strategy and focused on the older caucus goer." Part of the reason might be that the managing of Clinton's "likability" backfired with these voters as well. One Democratic strategist lamented: "Hillary became an icon and it hurt her and helped her. Everyone walked around saying, 'She's such a bitch.' They had to soften her image. She should have just been Hillary. The younger generation of voters appreciate the authentic nature of the person who is running."

CNN's Candy Crowley told me that it really struck her on the campaign trail that "younger women felt it was a much bigger deal to vote for a black man" but when it came to the women's movement, they "were unaware that the fight goes on."[13] Certainly Clinton herself tried to remind them that they were women, that they shared the same struggles and, in fact, their progress was a direct result of the battles her generation had fought and won.

Beginning with her own mother, Clinton frequently stumped with much older women by her side, using them as a way to visually underpin the historic nature of her campaign. The accompanying speeches invariably referred to the woman's advanced age—perhaps the Nineteenth Amendment had yet to be passed at the time the particular woman had been born and now, here they all were, less than a hundred years later, at a rally for the first woman candidate with a real possibility of getting the job that, at one time, the woman in question wasn't even enfranchised to vote for. That sort of thing. It was a nice history lesson, but this was a campaign—and campaigns are not a time for history lessons.

Clinton's campaign strategy didn't resonate with younger women. It didn't tap into their collective memory—suffrage had happened long before *they* were born—and it didn't tap into an emotional reservoir either. It was a bit like asking the average thirty-year-old to make an emotional connection to the moon landing—Neil Armstrong had made a giant leap for mankind, but they'd all read about it in their history books. They hadn't been around to watch the grainy black-and-white live coverage of it on some console TV.

But the sentiment expressed by Crowley—that it *was* a bigger deal to vote for a black man—was very prevalent, and it was certainly reflected in Obama's vote totals. That the sentiment was unsuccessfully countered seemed like a fundamental failure of both the traditional women's movement and the Clinton campaign. I can speculate that the reason for these failures went beyond the inability to move young women with a history lesson. Perhaps, like me, they were put off by the brashness and tired agendas of the women's rights advocates. Perhaps they were moving away from the idea of a "fight" and toward the concept of strategic empowerment that is one of the central ideas of this book.

The Clinton campaign had made a conscious decision to base its strategy on the female vote. It wasn't working, but nevertheless they stuck with it. This is a common error in presidential politics, that the strategy for the primary has to be married to the strategy for the general election. The Clinton campaign planned to run against a Republican man and expected to be the beneficiary of the historical gender gap that shows women voting for Democratic candidates in larger numbers.

The campaign had devised a strategy that depended on women as its very foundation but one that ignored, or could not effectively reach, young women. And the young voters—women and men—turned out in droves for Obama.

It seems fair to say that Clinton's people—and even Clinton herself—were totally caught off guard by the one-two punch of Obama's victory and her third-place finish in Iowa.

Clinton's camp tried to downplay the results in Iowa, claiming that she had always intended to focus only on primary states and discounted as unrepresentative of the Iowa Caucus process. But if that's true, it's a ridiculous strategy. Had Clinton put Obama away with an early and convincing win in Iowa, things would have almost certainly gone her way, something liberal reporters eagerly reported. The *Atlantic*'s Joshua Green pointed out,

> Even if she was presumed to be the heavy favorite, Clinton needed to win Iowa to maintain the impression of invincibility that she believed was her greatest advantage. And yet Iowa was a vulnerability. Both husband and wife lacked ties there: Bill Clinton had skipped the 1992 caucuses because Iowa's Senator Tom Harkin was running; in 1996, Clinton had run unopposed.[14]

If Clinton didn't care about Iowa, she had a funny way of showing it: by some estimates, Clinton, like Obama, reportedly spent $20 million there.[15]

The loss certainly did a few things. It robbed Clinton of her frontrunner status. Even worse, it hurt her ability to raise funds—already a growing concern. Perhaps most damaging for the long term, it proved that Obama was not just a viable candidate—he was viable in an overwhelmingly white state. People who had thought, "Hey, maybe he can really do this," now were beginning to believe it.

There was a silver lining: the loss in Iowa did allow Clinton to claim "comeback kid" status when she won the New Hampshire primary five days later with 39 percent to Obama's 36 percent. To say New Hampshire was a do-or-die win for Clinton is perhaps an overstatement, but only a slight one. It was a big win—and Clinton's victory in that state had been in doubt even before Obama's Iowa win. As recently as mid-December she had been locked in a dead heat with Obama, each receiving 32 percent of the vote (to Edwards's 18 percent) in a Gallup poll of likely New Hampshire Democratic primary voters.[16]

How much of Clinton's victory in New Hampshire could be attributed to her widely publicized "crying" incident in a Portsmouth coffee shop is debatable. Removed from the sentimental coverage it got in the press, in truth, Clinton never "cried." What she did was get a little misty, welling up with emotion that may or may not have been genuine but sure got a whole lot of airtime. And maybe it did serve to endear her to some people. But to attribute her primary victory to a teary chat with voters is a little too easy—and vastly oversimplified.

Still, another former Democratic White House official perceived it this way:

> I believe that when she showed her vulnerability in New Hampshire, women came to her defense. They won her the New Hampshire primary. We were ten points down in our internal polls the day before she cried in that diner. It turned around and she won. Mark [Penn] will tell you she won New Hampshire because it's when Hillary started attacking Obama. She attacked him in the debate. But I think that's horseshit. I think we won in spite of that. Hillary was never more popular than when she was perceived as a victim. Whether it be the Monica Lewinsky scandal, Gennifer Flowers or Whitewater. . . . It happened again in New Hampshire. . . . The massive political support. She didn't have money any more. . . . But what she did was kept fighting. And women came to her defense. They were passionate. They didn't have something to be passionate about prior to that moment.

Clinton had always been quite popular in New Hampshire and in nearby Massachusetts, a state that she would later win convincingly. And though she was down (or, by some accounting, even) in the polls, her supporters, I suspect, were perhaps more likely to get out and vote because they were quite likely to have been galvanized by her Iowa disaster. Plus, there was this: the last debate in New Hampshire, which occurred two days after Iowa and three days before the voting in New Hampshire. Clinton was very good in that debate—clear, direct, solid on the policy, and she even got a few laughs, as when she responded to a question about her personality—her "likability"—with a coy, "Well, that hurts my feelings . . . but I'll try to go on."[17]

Obama, as we all remember, responded with a terse: "You're likable enough, Hillary." And this dismissal may have hurt him as much as the "tears" helped her. As Richard Cohen wrote, it "was an ugly moment that showed a side of Obama we had not seen and it might not have been characteristic . . . and probably more than a few women recoiled from it."[18]

But whether it was Clinton's tears that were interpreted by some as a new show of likable human vulnerability that boosted her support, or Obama's curt dismissal that undermined, however briefly, *his* likability, Clinton won New Hampshire. But even though she won in that state—and recaptured the women's vote in a significant way—her campaign was never the same after Iowa. Her air of invincibility was gone; the inevitability of her candidacy was done. And, as has been widely reported, she burned through over $100 million by some estimates. That's a huge distraction in a campaign, especially when your opponent is not only flush but raising record sums each day. The Internet was Obama's cash cow and it had to have triggered some regret for Clinton that she hadn't incorporated better use of the technology into her own campaign. After all, she had to have known that, according to the Pew Internet & American Life Project, "More than men, women are enthusiastic online communicators." The audience was there, she just hadn't taken advantage of it—hadn't used it to reach either her target constituency or the young people for whom the Internet was a completely integrated and organic part of their lives—and that had to have hurt.

And then the claws came out. Not Hillary's. To her credit, in spite of whatever regrets or pressures were upon her, she continued to campaign in a dignified way to the end. But it was after Iowa that we saw some of the fiercest sexism of the campaign targeted at Senator Clinton. It was as if Hillary's detractors—and many pundits—reveled in her fall. And they couldn't help themselves from piling on in the most undignified ways possible.

There were the profane tee shirts—"Even Bill Wants Some-Booty Else!" and "Life's a Bitch, don't vote for one!" How about "Bitches Love Me" with the candidate caricatured with a dog's body, or the commentary "Unsubstantiated political rumor and innuendo has it that Hillary is going through Man-o-pause." There was the Hillary Nutcracker, advertised as having "stainless steel thighs" and able to crack the "toughest nuts"—not to mention that it was sold side-by-side with Corkscrew Bill, with a corkscrew for a penis—actual functional bar accessories for people with such juvenile senses of humor. There was even, from an organization that called itself "Militaria Press," a Hillary Rodham Clinton Urinal Target. Hillary's sex life, her marital status, and even rumors about her sexual orientation were fair game. These disgusting, tasteless products were contemptuous not of Hillary, but of the nation's highest office and the process America undertakes every four years to elect its leaders—but they were personally brutal too.

Still, I have to think that the more subtle attacks were even worse—and I know they were more damaging. Let's recall, first, Mark Rudov on Fox News on January 4, 2008, talking about Hillary's "nagging" voice: "When Barack Obama speaks, men hear, 'Take off for the future.' And when Hillary Clinton speaks, men hear, 'Take out the garbage.'" Or, how about Mike Barnicle's newsworthy contention on MSNBC's *Morning Joe* on January 23 that: "she reacts to [Senator Barack] Obama with just the look, the look toward him, looking like everyone's first wife standing outside a probate court."

We must not forget the stunning summation, as noted earlier, of Senator Clinton's professional career from Chris Matthews, who reminded us on January 9 the same year that "the reason she's a U.S. senator, the reason she's a candidate for President, the reason she may be a front runner, is that her husband messed around." These men weren't making statements as overtly tasteless as those on the tee shirts. They were engaging in the sort of talk publicly that is all too prevalent privately—talking about a woman in stereotypically derogatory terms. As if she were not a human being—and, in this case, a human being who was saying some important things that might well impact all of our futures. And no one was rising up to call them on it. Well, no one except informal "Hillary Sexism Watch" groups, like the one at Shakespeare's Sister blog that started keeping track in February of 2008 of the number of misogynistic attacks Hillary was subjected to—almost a year before the actual presidential election and well before the nomination process was anywhere near complete, there were already sixty-two separate incidents on their list.

The press certainly didn't keep a similar tally. No one reacted with real outrage. If anything, the media fed into it. When John McCain was asked by one of his followers how his campaign was going to "beat the bitch" when it came time for the general election, McCain, to what I believe was his ultimate detriment, didn't do the calling out himself. He laughed. And I had to believe that moment of laughter, captured on camera, did not do him any good when women decided whom to vote for in the general election. It wasn't the reason he lost, but it was the reason some potential voters lost faith in him.

But let's go back now to that Keith Olbermann comment I referenced earlier because it was truly the lowest point of the all the down-and-dirty things said about Clinton during the campaign. Olbermann was on the air, talking with one of his frequent guests, *Newsweek*'s Howard Fineman. They were discussing how a winner would ever be determined in a Democratic primary that seemed as if it were going to go on forever. Their supposition was that Clinton should step aside and concede the race to Obama. This idea ignored the fact that the *voters* were the ones who had given Clinton her right to continue to participate in that exercise in democracy we know as our nomination process. Fineman remarked that, in order to finally settle on the candidate he regarded as the rightful nominee—Obama—it was going to take "some adults somewhere in the Democratic party to step in [and] stop this thing, like a referee in a fight that could go on for thirty rounds. Those are the super, super, super delegates who are going to have to decide this."

Replied Olbermann: "Right. Somebody who can take her into a room and only he comes out."[19]

As Sklar wrote in her then-column on the Huffington Post:

What does that mean? Really, it can only mean one thing. Beating the crap out of Hillary Clinton, to the point where she is physically incapable of getting up and walking out. At minimum. We know this. We know this because we have all seen movies where people are invited into private places to have a "discussion" and the unruly party is, um, dealt with accordingly. It's an unmistakably violent image.

A violent, shattering image. And had it been a different candidate who had been the object of Olbermann's quote, the public would very likely have reacted to it with the appropriate outrage. As Sklar put it:

> There really seems to be only one interpretation [of Olbermann's comment] and the only point or debate is whether it's okay or not. I'm going to cut that one short: it's not. To the fellow (male) journo I wrote to about this yesterday, who waved it off as just some colorful film-noir imagery, I can say: can you IMAGINE if someone had said that about Obama? That he should be taken somewhere and dealt with, so that he wouldn't come back? Can you imagine if some right-winger had talked about getting Obama out of the race "the old-fashioned way"? If that last one makes you cringe, it should, because it evokes a history of violence against black people in this country that is raw and real. Well, frankly, the same goes for women—many of whom have been taken somewhere private and never returned.[20]

What may be even more bizarre than Olbermann's comment was the reaction to it: nothing. No public outcry. No wrist slapping of Olbermann—no standard apology issued amid threats of suspension from his job (however insincere those sorts of forced apologies always are), no statement from his bosses at MSNBC distancing themselves from either the statement or the withering sentiment behind it.

Even more curious, in light of the nonreaction to Olbermann's statement, was the *over*reaction to a statement by MSNBC's David Shuster who made the on-air remark in February 2008, in reference to Clinton's daughter's joining her on the campaign trail, "doesn't it seem like Chelsea's sort of being pimped out in some weird sort of way?"

Now, let's state for the record that candidates' children often campaign for their parents. In 2008 alone we saw Mike Huckabee's daughter Sarah acting as her father's field manager, Meghan McCain blogging on her father's behalf, and Cate Edwards as well as all those Romney boys out on the stump for their fathers. Children on the hustings are not out of the ordinary in any sense. And let's put aside that, indeed, it seemed that Chelsea was not persuaded to join her mother's campaign until late in the game, when it couldn't escape the notice of any seasoned pol that Clinton's camp was at last trying to appeal to women in Chelsea's age group. But what does "pimp" mean? It's just a hip term for promoting or advertising a product. Even Sklar, who by all accounts lost her job over her unstoppable outrage at Olbermann's violent proposal and her defense of Clinton in the face of it, believed that Shuster's gravest gaffe was that "at one moment in time he thought he was being hip. That's it!"

In contrast to the Olbermann fiasco, however, Shuster apologized for the words he chose to use—"I used a phrase that was inappropriate and I apologize to the Clinton family, the Clinton campaign and all of you who are justifiably offended"—*and* he was suspended from his job.

Can you conjure up in your mind what would have happened had Shuster referred to Obama's "pimping" his two central-casting-cute little daughters? The racist overtone would have been unavoidable—as would have been the consequences of making a racist insinuation.

*P*ERHAPS, HOWEVER, most interesting of all were the reactions to NBC's Lester Holt when it was reported that he seemed a bit too incredulous when discussing Clinton's clear lead over Obama on the "commander in chief" question:

> With the field of Democratic candidates reduced to two, we asked primary voters, "Who would make the best commander in

chief of the U.S. armed forces?" And here, it was [Sen.] Hillary Clinton [D-NY] who was the clear favorite. The first woman candidate with a serious shot at winning the presidency beat out her male rival—look at these numbers—50 percent to 30 percent. Keep in mind, this at a time the nation is fighting on two fronts.[21]

Was it a moment of ill-advised humor, or of being caught off guard by an inappropriate comment on the campaign trail and trying to brush it off with laughter?

In fact, it was a profoundly telling moment, that however far down the road we think women have come to equality, we may not be there yet. Granted, live television's a high-wire act. We've all made the blunder we wish we could take back. Unfortuantely, these spontaneous outbursts override the substance of the news story, which in this case was profound.

And then there was the infamous "iron my shirt" incident.

On January 7, 2008, on one of Clinton's final campaign stops before the New Hampshire primary, two men stood up in the school auditorium where she was speaking and started shouting, "Iron my shirt!" at her—the same slogan that was on the signs they raised. Clinton kept her cool, remarking, "Ah the remnants of sexism, alive and well," to the applause of her audience before cueing up the lights so police could see to come and take the two hecklers away. "As I think has been abundantly demonstrated, I am also running to break through the highest and hardest glass ceiling," she continued, on a sober note, though at the end of her speech she was composed enough to jest, as the question and answer portion of the program got underway, "If there's anyone left in the auditorium who wants to learn how to iron a shirt, I'll talk about that."[22]

The incident made the news, of course, but it didn't cause outrage, at least not in the general population. One blog actually tried to brush it off as a harmless prank connected to a couple of kids who wanted to generate some publicity for their radio show, noting that one of the perpetrators, a "Nick Gemelli, who is 21, and born at least a decade after 'iron my shirts' was an anti–women's rights slogan, didn't have much of a rationale. 'I just don't think a woman should be president,' he said." Some others had the temerity to suggest that the kids who pulled it off were plants by the Clinton campaign itself to drum up their own publicity. Even Candy Crowley demurred on this one: "I saw the two boys in New Hampshire . . . hold the sign 'iron my shirts' or whatever. It didn't strike me as intrinsically sexist. It struck me as intrinsically stupid."[23]

But let's forget, for a moment, that one of the things we all should have been fuming about was that a couple of smart-aleck kids were asking a United States senator to do their laundry. The disrespect to the office should have automatically triggered our ire no matter the gender of the senator involved.

Imagine what might have happened in the press if the scenario had been just a little different. What if the incident had taken place during the recent election of the new chairman of the Republican National Party? What if, during one of Michael Steele's speeches, these two young men had stood up and started waving signs and shouting at him the slogan "Shine my shoes"?

Did you suddenly feel a looming silence? Did the room just feel a little colder?

My bet is that, if "Shine my shoes" had been the slogan of the day, it would have galvanized us as a community and fomented protests in a way that just didn't happen when Clinton was asked to iron shirts. In a way, that couldn't happen because she is a woman and, as a culture, we don't yet take sexism nearly to heart the way we do racism and other forms of prejudice.

This is not to say that nobody was ticked off. It was in the aftermath of these attacks that we saw legions of women—particularly middle-aged and older, low-to-moderate-income, white and Hispanic women—rise up in defense of Hillary. This was the birth of what Senator Clinton would later dub "the Sisterhood of the

Traveling Pantsuits" in her speech to the Democratic National Convention in Denver.[24]

As Margaret Doris would later write in *Esquire,* to these women,

> Hillary Clinton achieved national political credibility *despite* the fact that she was forced to abandon her last name and adopt her husband's so he could run for president, *because* she was reviled for being too smart, *because* she made it her business to make her place in places they said she didn't belong, *because* she stuck up for a husband who turned out to be a liar, and not only for giving up almost everything for a man's ambitions but for finally having a chance to get it back. These women get it. They get her.[25]

Hillary's life experience was deeply moving to women of her own generation—those women who had lived it too—and they rallied for her.

But even with more passionate support from her most loyal supporters, the damage was done. Clinton was locked in a battle with Obama that, it seemed increasingly probable, she would lose. And to some, her staying in the race was hurting the Democratic Party and draining resources from both candidates. Bearing this out were Hillary's unfavorability ratings. They were already high, owing to her years in the public eye and the contempt bred by familiarity with a person who—often by virtue of her sex alone—roused controversy, but they continued to climb pretty dramatically.

In mid-April 2008, an ABC News–*Washington Post* poll reported that "54 percent of respondents said they have an *unfavorable* view of Senator Clinton, up from 40 percent a few days after she'd won the New Hampshire primary in early January. Her favorability rating had fallen among both Democrats and independents over the past three months." It was now at the highest level "at any time since the *Post* and ABC began asking the question, in 1992."[26] The reason for this precipitous drop seemed pretty clear: Clinton was obstinately refusing to give up the primary challenge. Interestingly, though, the same poll found that most Democrats—nearly 60 percent—who were aligned with one of the candidates "said they would prefer to see Clinton and Obama continue campaigning until one of them wins a clear victory, rather than bringing the fight to an early conclusion."

The longer Hillary stayed in, the more unfavorably she was viewed. But, then again, folks weren't quite ready for her to quit the race either; and they still saw her as the more experienced of the two. This paradox is partially attributable to the length of the campaign; as people get to know you, the sheen wears off. Obama's unfavorables were rising too, though not as much and nowhere near as fast. But let's also at least entertain the notion that the reason Hillary's numbers were skidding could be a result of the uncomfortable idea that voters instinctively have less tolerance for a female candidate in "attack mode." And Hillary was undeniably in attack mode—indeed, she was fighting for her political life.

Lest we forget, the Democratic primary debates showcased the growing tension between the two "first of their kind" candidates—and made for some memorable exchanges, each candidate seeming to vie for who was most irritated with the other. The debate in South Carolina just two weeks before Super Tuesday included some fairly below-the-belt jabs. First Clinton knocked Obama with, "Well, you know, Senator Obama, it is very difficult having a straight-up debate with you, because you never take responsibility for any vote, and that has been a pattern." Obama responded by throwing back this punch, in reference to Clinton's seeming to deploy her husband, the former president, as her surrogate to attack him, "I can't tell who I'm running against sometimes." Obama's counterpunch was effective. Its effect was to immediately remind voters of the fact that Clinton had already spent eight years in the White House, albeit as the second half of her husband's 1992 "two for one" deal. It was a subtle yet unmistakable reminder that she was the Washington insider, and he was the agent of change in this election season.

In the April 16 debate in Philadelphia—which came just six days before the all-important Pennsylvania primary—Clinton came out swinging. She might have stumbled over her explanation of misspeaking about sniper fire on a tarmac in Bosnia, but the moderator, ABC's Charles Gibson, wasted no time in bringing up Obama's connection to the controversial pastor Jeremiah Wright. Obama dismissed those sorts of associations as mere distractions from the real issues that real people cared about, and Clinton jumped on it, insisting that all such associations would be fodder for the no-holds-barred general election that lay ahead. Among the arsenal she had on hand that night, Clinton had new ammunition: her fight for blue-collar voters, and she made Obama labor over that as well, trying to explain it during the Philadelphia debate. And then there was Obama's offhand comment at a San Francisco fundraiser about "bitter" voters who "cling to guns or religion or antipathy to people who aren't like them."

Having already apologized for the remark, and perhaps frustrated by the staying power of the words he'd thought he was sharing in a more confidential setting, Obama tried to turn the attack around as more "politics as usual." He said: "So the problem that we have in our politics, which is fairly typical, is that you take one person's statement, if it's not properly phrased, and you just beat it to death. . . . And that's what Senator Clinton's been doing over the last four days." To make his point very clear, Obama didn't hesitate to bring up the fact that Clinton had made her own share of unfortunate remarks. Obama chose to use the infamous "cookie" exchange from way back in 1992 as his example, saying: "You know, I recall when back in 1992, when she made a statement about how, 'what do you expect, should I be at home baking cookies?' And people attacked her for being elitist and this and that. And I remember watching that on TV and saying, well, that's not who she is; that's not what she believes; that's not what she meant. And I'm sure that that's how she felt as well."

For all of Obama's quick comebacks, Clinton was seen as victorious. The *New York Times* called it "arguably one of Mr. Obama's weakest debate performances," pointing out that he "at times appeared annoyed." By contrast, according to the *Times,* "Mrs. Clinton appeared, for the most part, calm and in control, particularly when the discussion moved to such questions as how the two candidates would respond to an attack by Iran on Israel and whether they would promise not to raise taxes as president."[27]

Clinton went on to win the Pennsylvania primary, of course. And she would compete in all the remaining primaries before she finally bowed out of the race on June 7 and threw her support behind Obama, encouraging her supporters to do the same: "I ask all of you to join me in working as hard for Barack Obama as you have for me."[28]

After her speech, Obama released a statement saying, "Obviously, I am thrilled and honored to have Senator Clinton's support. But more than that, I honor her today for the valiant and historic campaign she has run. She shattered barriers on behalf of my daughters and women everywhere, who now know that there are no limits to their dreams. And she inspired millions with her strength, courage and unyielding commitment to the cause of working Americans."

So, that was that, right? Not so fast. Clinton continued to be dogged by claims of "too little, too late"—that she didn't do enough (and not soon enough) to support Obama.

At the Democratic National Convention in Denver, a largely manufactured drama over whether Clinton's name would be entered into nomination petered out when Clinton moved to nominate Obama by acclamation. And during her speech, she was pretty clear about where she stood: "I am honored to be here tonight. A proud mother. A proud Democrat. A proud American. And a proud supporter of Barack Obama. My friends, it is time to take back the country we love. Whether you voted for me, or voted for Barack, the time is now to unite as a single party with a single purpose. We are on the same team, and none of us can sit on the sidelines. . . . Barack Obama is my candidate. And he must be our President."[29]

HILLARY AND THE B-WORD

No, not that B-word. *Bitter.* Throughout the campaign and even after her concession and her convention speech, Clinton was blasted as a bitter sore loser. The blogs were particularly ruthless: "Hillary Clinton, Vice-President Sore Loser," from Kelly McParland, on National Post (June 4, 2008). "Hillary Clinton—Loser? Sore Loser? Or Both?" from Gary A. Johnson's BlackMenIn America.com blog, in which he wrote: "I wouldn't put her on the ticket. I don't trust her. Yes, I said it. Hillary Clinton would not be my Vice President. I don't believe that she is genetically capable of being Vice President Clinton to President Obama."

This image was, of course, immortalized hilariously by Amy Poehler on *Saturday Night Live,* in which her "Hillary" quipped: "Sore loser, racist supporters, no ethical standards. Qualities Senator Obama simply cannot match. That's not an attack on my opponent. It's just the truth. When you consider that, the choice is obvious."[30]

Clinton's supporters—or, more precisely, her female supporters—were dubbed bitter as well. The *Economist* contributed "Mrs. Clinton's bitter supporters." And there was "Defeat leaves a bitter taste for Hillary Clinton's female supporters" from the *Daily Telegraph.* Men did indeed vote for Hillary Clinton. But they weren't accused of bitterness. This continued even after Hillary campaigned heavily for Obama—including in battleground states like Florida (where both Clintons are extremely popular). But it still wasn't enough to convince some that she was over it.

Her old "friend" Dick Morris along with Eileen McGann offered in August 2008 that "it would be a mistake to think that Hillary's campaign against Obama is over. She and Bill both realize that if McCain wins, she would be the likely Democratic nominee against him in 2012. . . . In public, they will appear to be his biggest fans. . . . [But] Hillary will do her best to avoid campaigning for Obama and will undercut him in any way she can without getting caught. Obama: Watch your back!"[31]

Now some of this logically resulted from a terrifically long, incredibly expensive, very passionate primary campaign that was toughly fought on both sides. Hard feelings are natural and inevitable—and deeply felt. Supporters pour their money, their time, and their hopes into a candidate—and they're justifiably heartbroken when it doesn't work out.

The difference is: we don't see this vitriolic, conniving "bitterness" charge lodged at men and their supporters. Was Mike Huckabee a bitter sore loser? Was Rudy Giuliani bitter? Was John Edwards? You know what? They probably were. All losing candidates probably harbor some bitterness, or at least a little sense of "it should've been me." But are they portrayed that way? Of course not.

And that, perhaps, is the final hurdle we have yet to overcome. Hillary Clinton proved she could get the votes nationally; she could raise the money—or at least *a lot* of money. But she was still subject to the divisive, undercutting power of sexism.

Katie Couric opined during her *CBS Evening News* broadcast on June 11, 2008, "One of the great lessons of [Hillary Clinton's] campaign is the continued and accepted role of sexism in American life, particularly in the media. . . . It isn't just Hillary Clinton who needs to learn a lesson from this primary season—it's all the people who crossed the line, and all the women and men who let them get away with it."[32] One of those who got away with it? Again, Keith Olbermann. And he not only got away with it, he rubbed women's faces in it, naming Couric the "worst person in the world" for "her own promulgation of the nonsense that Senator Clinton was a victim of sexism."

Let's be clear: sexism wasn't the overriding reason she lost. Give credit where credit is due. Her opponent was better by nearly every measure—he had better organization on the ground and more flexibility; a better campaign strategy and operational structure; a far superior fundraising operation via the Internet; much better use of his personal story; a more inspirational message; and he was more convincing on the issues that mattered to people.

As CNN senior political correspondent Candy Crowley pointed out when I asked her: "yes, there was an undercurrent of sexism" throughout the campaign, "but that's not the reason Hillary Clinton lost."[33]

I think Crowley's observation is accurate, though I also agree with her that there are just more expectations of woman candidates than of their male counterparts—not the least being, as I have pointed out, a woman must not only be competent, she must be likable. And, much as I have decried and will continue to decry the focus on a woman candidate's physical appearance, Crowley offers us one more story that speaks to the unique pressure on a female running for office:

> I think part of the way [Clinton] is has to do with her experience in public life. She's guarded and anyone could understand [that] given her experience. At one point I was going to interview her on the CNN bus. We were in Iowa. It was so freaking cold, and she had to walk about two hundred yards and it was so windy. She gets on and her hair looks all crazy. I said, "Senator, would you like to take a look in our mirror?" She says, "Oh, yes, yes." She goes over to the mirror. She opens this mirror and it's about three feet by three feet. It is lit up like a baseball stadium. The lights are insane. She opens up this thing and the lights go on. She says, "Oh, now, that's scary." It was totally an "I get it moment."
>
> I think she's talked publicly about this. The sheer logistics of being a woman candidate. John Kerry or Barack Obama can roll out of bed, step out of the shower, put on the same suit and walk out. If you're Hillary Clinton, you can't put on the same suit. Somebody has to do your hair or people are going to talk about how tired you look that day. I think about this with male correspondents all the time. It takes me two hours to go on the air. They are calling, saying, "How soon can you be on air?" Well, the boys run right upstairs and go on air because that's acceptable. I have to go put makeup on because it would not be ac-

ceptable for me to be on air without makeup. And it would not be acceptable for Hillary Clinton to go someplace without makeup. So, logistically, it's very tough. Why? Because people have expectations from their female candidates. They want them to look good. That adds another two hours to the day. It's significant when you are racing across the country.

We place a unique pressure on our female candidates. Even in the absence of outright sexism, it is nevertheless significant.

Though we can't say how much it affected the outcome, there's no denying that sexism happened, it mattered, and it was ugly. As Clinton herself explained it, as her campaign was winding down:

> It's been deeply offensive to millions of women. . . . The manifestation of some of the sexism that has gone on in this campaign is somehow more respectable, or at least more accepted, and . . . there should be equal rejection of the sexism and the racism when it raises its ugly head. It does seem as though the press at least is not as bothered by the incredible vitriol that has been engendered by the comments by people who are nothing but misogynists.[34]

Hillary Clinton wasn't the only one to feel it.

2

THE PALIN EFFECT

$\mathcal{C}$OUNTLESS OBSERVERS OF THE 2008 presidential election concluded that Sarah Palin was simply a bad vice presidential choice—unprepared for both the rigors of the campaign and the awesome duties of the vice presidency and, possibly, the presidency. To these voters, she was a drain on the Republican ticket.

The day-to-day tracking polls do not bear this out. In fact, there was a bump in support that lasted until September 15, when Lehman Brothers collapsed and the bottom fell out of the economy. The McCain-Palin ticket never recovered from this precipitous and constant decline in support, which resulted in the seven-point popular vote defeat on the election date.

Unlike Senator Hillary Clinton, who was a political powerhouse with one of the most recognizable names in American politics, Sarah Palin entered the arena as a relative unknown.

But Palin did have her fans. Still in her first term, Palin had been elected governor of Alaska only after running against, and beating, incumbent Republican Frank Murkowski. The campaign to draft her for vice president may have begun has early as February 2007 when Adam Brickley, a former Heritage Foundation intern, put PalinforVP.blogpost.com up on the Internet.

Brickley, after some consideration of the disastrous results the GOP experienced in the 2006 election, came to the conclusion that, for the Republicans to retain the White House in 2008, they needed to make a radical break with party tradition. To Brickley, that break was to put a woman in the No. 2 slot on the national ticket.

Dismissing Republican senators Kay Bailey Hutchison of Texas and Olympia Snowe of Maine as too moderate, Brickley settled on Palin, who was quietly establishing a reputation for competent and conservative governance in the nation's forty-ninth state. Conservative Web sites like InstaPundit and American Scene took notice, and the chase was on. They helped promote the idea of a Palin candidacy that eventually reached mainstream conservative media outlets when the *American Spectator* and, later, Rush Limbaugh signed on as Palin supporters.

In the summer of 2007, Palin entertained two groups of prominent conservative thinkers at the governor's mansion in Juneau. Two well-known conservative magazines—Rupert Murdoch's *Weekly Standard,* and the *National Review,* founded by conservative icon William F. Buckley and now edited by a young conservative named Rich Lowry—had each organized luxury cruises to Alaska for politically minded vacationers with magazine staffers—writers and editors—tasked with giving lectures to the ships' guests. When the ships stopped in Alaska, the writers and editors made a stop for lunch with Palin. These pundits included Fred Barnes, the co-host of Fox News's *The Beltway Boys,* Victor Davis Hanson, a historian with particularly close ties to Vice President Dick Cheney, and William Kristol, the television talking head who founded Murdoch's *Weekly Standard* and was, at the time, also an op-ed columnist for the *New York Times*.

The vacationing pundits' embrace of Palin was nearly immediate. But what is most interesting about the tenor is the way these men—and they were, all of them, men—reacted to her over these luncheons. It was not that they were impressed by her intelligence or her confidence—and they let it be known that they were, indeed, impressed by both. What is intriguing is Barnes's assertion that, in addition to being "struck by how smart Palin was and how unusually confident," he also noted that she was "exceptionally pretty."

It is worth noting, and especially germane to the discussion we're having in this book, that Hanson recalled that on the day of their luncheon, Palin was wearing high heels. And in championing Palin to be McCain's vice presidential running mate, Kristol referred to her in an interview on Fox News as "my heartthrob."

Jay Nordlinger, a senior editor at *National Review* who also met with Palin, summed up the general consensus in his online column, writing of Palin that she was "a former beauty pageant contestant, and a real honey, too. Am I allowed to say that? Probably not, but too bad."

It is indeed too bad. Even before Palin had been chosen as McCain's running mate, the sexualization of her candidacy had already begun. And by the very people who were most eager to see her on the ticket because they were sure that her inclusion on the ticket—her smarts and her confidence—would help McCain win the presidency. However genuinely these men might have meant their observations of Palin's physical attributes as compliments, they were already subtly setting the stage for her political attributes and her record as governor to be taken less seriously than her good looks.

For confirmation of this assertion, let's take a brief look at some of the words that were used in the press at the time that Palin was just being introduced to the country as its possible next vice president:

> Alaska Gov. Sarah Palin—a former high school basketball star, beauty queen . . .
> —Wayne Slater, "Election '08 President,"
> *Dallas Morning News,* 7/26/08

> A former beauty queen . . .
> —William E. Gibson, "Finding the Perfect Fit,"
> Fort Lauderdale *Sun-Sentinel,* 7/20/08

a happily married mother of five who is . . . drop dead gorgeous . . .

—Jack Kelly, "McCain's Secret Weapon,"
Pittsburgh Post-Gazette, 6/8/08

The objectification of Palin started early, and, because of it—because she was touted as a "beauty queen," usually cultural shorthand for "dumb" and, one of my other favorite words, "bimbo"—it was much easier for the mainstream press to begin to peg her as incompetent.

This is one of the problems that I am trying to help to puzzle out with this book: the impact a woman's physical being has on our political acceptance, or non-acceptance, of what she stands for. Let's be fair: Ronald Reagan was known for his shock of still-boyish brown hair. John Edwards's hairstyle similarly drew our attention—along with the costly haircuts that he enjoyed to manage it and that helped undercut his image as an advocate for the working class—remember "the two Americas"?[1] JFK's impish grin and rugged good looks were much commented on during his time in the White House and, over forty years after his death, his youthful vigor is still a large part of the public's perception of that charismatic president.

But would a commentator ever make a remark about the sexy footwear of George W. Bush or call John F. Kerry a honey? Just wouldn't have happened. Try, if you will, to imagine this scenario: It's 2004, and Dee Dee Myers and I are doing a guest spot on CNN, commenting as a conservative paired with a liberal on the presidential race. And Wolf Blitzer turns to us to ask, "How will each of the candidates' foreign policy philosophies impact our strained relations with Iran?" Try to imagine, if you possibly can, Dee Dee Myers saying somewhere in her answer that Kerry's being "a real honey" would help ease tensions between the two nations. Everyone would have said that Dee Dee had lost it. The same would have been true if I had made some comment about the manliness of W's cowboy boots setting the stage for tough negotiations with the world's leading sponsor of state-backed terror.

In either case, these comments, while being somewhat beside the point, would have been seen as reflecting badly on us as analysts—sort of like the way MSNBC's Chris Matthews was ridiculed for a comment about Barack Obama's speech giving him a "thrill" going up his leg.[2]

It was not long before Palin started to receive regular mention as a possible McCain pick—even if a long-shot one—but the focus on her looks continued. The Florida *Sun-Sentinel* described Palin this way in July 2008: "A former beauty queen, Palin is the tough-minded Republican governor of Alaska, famed for riding snowmobiles and eating moose burgers. Like McCain, she is a maverick Republican willing to work with Democrats. This forty-four-year-old rising star would bring youth and glamour to the Republican ticket."[3] The *Pittsburgh Post-Gazette* described her as "both the youngest and the first female governor in Alaska's relatively brief history as a state. She's also the most popular governor in America, with an approval rating that has bounced around 90 percent. . . . Fire and nice. A happily married mother of five who is smart and drop dead gorgeous."[4]

Palin is clearly unusual. As blogger Nate Silver, the creator of Fivethirtyeight.com, has written, "Alaska isn't the first place you'd expect to see a woman elected to higher office. With its harsh climate and reliance on traditionally male-dominated industries like fishing, mining, and oil extraction, it has the most male population in the country: 106 men for every 100 women."[5] And yet it has an ultra-popular woman governor, one who is treated with a degree of seriousness at home but who is objectified by the national media.

It's intriguing, if not irritating, to see how they handle a female candidate's looks, while discounting her professional accomplishments—usually to the disadvantage of whatever party she is running with. And sometimes it's just as intriguing and irritating to see how a woman's appearance can be used against an opponent. Hillary Clinton, a woman now in her sixties—while not Hollywood glamorous—is not unattractive. She's not an actress, she's an accomplished politician—we don't expect "glamour" from her any more than we expect it of other candidates—or do we?

It strains credibility to think that conservative outlets routinely chose to run with the most unflattering photos of Clinton out of either innocence or a lack of more flattering shots to choose among. Rush Limbaugh, speaking of a particularly unflattering photo of Clinton taken on a freezing New Hampshire evening after a long day on the campaign trail, asked: "Will Americans want to watch a woman get older before their eyes on a daily basis?" But the same extraordinary phenomenon—human aging—was one Limbaugh dismissed as insignificant for male candidates because men as they age look "more authoritative, accomplished and distinguished."

He may not be alone in thinking like this; in fact, there are lots of women who will say the same thing, at least about men and women as a general rule. But can we be blamed for feeling a little discomforted that a woman who looked her age on the campaign trail was somehow disqualified from higher office while Fred Thompson's jowls make him look more presidential? It was a clear case of a double standard and it was infuriating and—until Hillary Clinton's campaign made an issue of it—it flew almost completely under the radar.

Consider Limbaugh's take on pretty old men/ugly old women with his enthusiasm for the (now) forty-four-year-old (but someday, if she's lucky, to be sixty-year-old) Palin: "Sarah Palin: babies, guns, Jesus. Hot damn!"

And contrast Limbaugh's take on Palin's man appeal, too, with Mike Barnicle's take on Clinton's: "she reacts the way she reacts to [Senator Barack] Obama with just the look, the look toward him, looking like everyone's first wife standing outside a probate court."

Here's Limbaugh's exchange with a caller on Palin:

Limbaugh: She's not shrill.
Caller: Right.

Limbaugh: She's not going to remind anybody of their ex-wife, she's going to remind men, "Gee, I wish she was single."
Caller: Exactly.[6]

Did Limbaugh believe he was issuing Palin a compliment? Did he believe that his comments would increase Palin's credibility on the issues that voters cared about? If he did, *why* did he believe it? Could it have been that he, like McCain, was playing by the same old patriarchal rules that even Clinton, however unwittingly, had been playing by? Could it have been that Limbaugh, like McCain, believed that a *show* of changing the rules—inviting a woman to be part of the team—would suffice for *substance*—allowing her to actually play the game? Whatever it was the men who promoted or handled Palin believed, they were wrong. And they got her off to an awfully bad start.

A May 2008 *New York Times* article about possible female presidential candidates entitled "She Just Might Be President Some Day" helpfully explained that the first woman to be president will come "from the South," and will be "a Democrat who has won in a red state" or, most surprisingly of all, "a Republican who has emerged from the private sector to run for governor." Apparently the *New York Times,* and everyone else for that matter, thought a successful governor with a 90 percent plus approval rating might actually be able to make a national run for the White House.

The occasional mention—and dismissal—notwithstanding, Palin was so new to the vast majority of Americans when McCain announced her as his running mate that we had to be told how to pronounce her name—"Note to Nation: Palin Rhymes with Van Halen," said the *Juneau Empire.*

Her biography and accomplishments became known soon enough, and not necessarily on the schedule Palin or the McCain campaign might have liked. But the announcement of her candidacy prompted immediate speculation about why McCain had chosen her. In one sense, this is the normal course of events: analyze the veep selection, explain the greater meaning to the general public. But then the speculation began.

Could it have been concern about how Alaska's all-important three electoral votes might go? Nah. Was there a strong personal connection between McCain and Palin that we heretofore didn't know about? Nope. McCain had not spent more than a total of three hours with Palin before he chose her to share his ticket. Okay, then, was it a kinship among "mavericks," something McCain recognized during that three-hour meeting? Not according to sources high up in the Republican campaign.

Then it must have been purely a gender play, a reach to disaffected "Hillary voters" who might be persuaded to cross over to the GOP. Or McCain's belief that Palin's nomination would unify a still distrustful Republican base.

In truth, it was probably some combination of those factors plus one more: McCain *desperately* needed to do *something* to shake up the race. Well, he sure did.

Out of the gate the Palin choice looked golden, inspired, just the kind of right move that clinches victories. In early September, with Palin now on the ticket, polls showed McCain battling back to a dead heat with Obama. Gallup's Daily Tracking Poll of registered voters (which was conducted every day but consolidated into three-day averages), showed a dramatic turnaround for McCain-Palin. In the period between September 2 and 4, Obama was polling at 48 percent to McCain's 44 percent; between September 5 and 7 those numbers had completely flipped, with Obama at 44 percent and McCain at 48 percent.[7]

On September 9, an ABC News–*Washington Post* poll had McCain at 49 percent to Obama's 47 percent (with a three-point margin of error). Most telling: the swing in support was attributed to women voters, especially white women. "White women had shifted from an eight-point pre-convention edge for Obama to a whopping twelve-point McCain advantage." Among white women polled, *58 percent* "said McCain's choice for vice president makes them more confident in the types of decisions he would make as president."

Among women polled in late July for Lifetime Networks' "Every Woman Counts" campaign, on the question of "understanding women and what is most important to them," they had agreed that "Barack Obama handily beat John McCain 52 percent to 18 percent [with 11 percent saying 'neither]. . . . Just six weeks later, and with the addition of Sarah Palin to the Republican ticket, McCain/Palin has dramatically reversed those fortunes, now in a virtual tie with Obama/Biden, 44 percent to 42 percent."[8] Dramatic reversal indeed!

Moreover, Palin—and the entire Republican National Convention—managed to boost the level of excitement among Republicans (especially conservatives) in exactly the way that was needed if McCain and Palin were to have any hope of winning the White House.

According to the same ABC News–*Washington Post* poll, "for the first time since the end of the primaries, a majority of voters are enthusiastic about McCain's candidacy, and the percentage calling themselves 'very enthusiastic' has nearly doubled from late August. That percentage is drastically higher now *among conservative Republicans and white evangelical Protestants*" (emphasis added).[9]

It was the big shake-up that Republicans had hoped for—more than just your typical convention bounce. But it wasn't sustained. The question is, why?

By most accounts Palin's speech at the GOP convention was a big win for the Republicans. Her ratings were huge. According to Nielsen, more than 37.2 million people tuned in for coverage of the third night of the GOP convention, which featured Palin. This was about a million shy of Barack Obama's record-breaking speech on day four of the Democratic convention. Women, in particular, watched in large numbers: 19.5 million overall, which was 5.2 million more women than had watched Hillary Clinton address the Democratic convention and 6.9 million more women than watched Joe Biden accept the Democrats' vice presidential nomination.[10]

With her telegenic family present in the hall, Palin told the nation who she was; she connected her personal story to her policy convictions; she made an argument for her managerial experience, her reformer credentials, and her ability "to challenge the status quo, to serve the common good, and to leave this nation better than we found it;" and she came out swinging for her candidate—John McCain ("a true profile in courage").

Palin showed that she wasn't going to be shy about going on the attack. She said bluntly that Obama "wants to forfeit" in Iraq and, in one of the more frequently quoted lines of the night, said:

> I guess a small-town mayor is sort of like a "community organizer," except that you have actual responsibilities. I might add that in small towns, we don't quite know what to make of a candidate who lavishes praise on working people when they are listening, and then talks about how bitterly they cling to their religion and guns when those people aren't listening. We tend to prefer candidates who don't talk about us one way in Scranton and another way in San Francisco.[11]

Palin showed right up front that she was willing to pull out all the stops to get her point across. But she also did something else; she made a direct and personal play for female voters, saying, "among the many things I owe [my parents] is one simple lesson: that this is America, and every woman can walk through every door of opportunity."

This was a direct appeal to Clinton voters who were disappointed that their candidate—the person in whom they'd invested the hope for the first woman president—had lost. It was no secret that many of these Clinton supporters could be said to be disenchanted with the Democratic Party for the disrespect it had shown to an experienced and well-qualified woman—and perhaps the best-qualified candidate in the race—in favor of yet another male candidate. Palin was signaling to them in her acceptance speech that she was ready to be the one that, at last, shattered that final glass ceiling.

And the kudos began to pour in as soon as the speech was over. CNN's Wolf Blitzer called it "an amazing speech from the Republican vice presidential candidate" and predicted "A star is born." NBC's Tom Brokaw thought she "could not have been more winning and engaging." On ABC's *Nightline,* George Stephanopoulos said, "She definitely gets an A. . . . It was appealing and funny and warm at times. Very, very tough at times as well. And she really did have an ability to bring these things down to earth." The *New York Times* proclaimed: "Palin Assails Critics and Electrifies Party."

More than a few Democratic strategists and pundits spent sleepless nights after that speech. On CBS, Joe Trippi said Palin "passed this test with flying colors," though he added a caveat: "but this one was controlled, a crowd that adored her with a teleprompter. Now she has to go out, face the press, answer their questions, see how she does against Joe Biden. But if you are the Democrats right now, you're taking this thing a lot more seriously."[12]

Wrote Camille Paglia, a dissident feminist and, as she puts it, a "stubborn" Democrat, on Salon.com,

> Pow! Wham! The Republicans unleashed a doozy—one of the most stunning surprises that I have ever witnessed in my adult life. . . . I had heard vaguely about Palin but had never heard her speak. I nearly fell out of my chair. It was like watching a boxing match or a quarter of hard-hitting football. . . . This woman turned out to be a tough, scrappy fighter with a mischievous sense of humor.[13]

The backlash began almost as immediately as the praise had started, and what we were hearing from people who wanted to downplay Palin's impact was a lot about how terrific her speechwriters were. It was as if to say: "Remember folks: she was great and all, but she didn't actually write that speech herself; the boys helped her out." Well, let's be frank: though all political speech writers are not "boys"—Peggy Noonan comes instantly to mind— virtually all politicians, male and female, employ speech writers. It was quite possibly Abraham Lincoln himself, scratching out the Gettysburg Address on the back of an envelope while riding to

Pennsylvania, who was the last president to pen the words he would pronounce behind the podium without help.

My point is that, at this stage of the McCain-Palin campaign, before America really knew Palin at all, there was already the inclination to dismiss her because she was a woman, and a woman couldn't possibly have put together a powerful speech like that on her own. It didn't matter that she had delivered it powerfully; what mattered, it seemed, was that she hadn't written it. I don't remember hearing criticism after Joe Biden's convention speech that he too had used a speechwriter. Nor, for that matter, based on his past behavior, that he may have plagiarized it.

Still, no one was writing her off, of course. That would come later, after the planeloads of national Democratic operatives and political reporters descended on tiny Wasilla, Alaska. For the moment, America was still getting to know Palin and trying to figure out what her nomination would mean to the Republican ticket—and to the outcome of the election.

As Ron Nessen, the former Ford White House press secretary now with the Brookings Institution, put it, "John McCain's selection of Alaska Gov. Sarah Palin as his vice presidential running mate was a surprise; possibly, a rare good surprise." He pointed out that Palin effectively "neutralizes Obama's message that he and his running mate Joe Biden represent 'change.'" The McCain-Palin ticket, he said, "teams a presidential candidate sometimes referred to as a 'maverick,' who often opposes his party's positions on major issues, with a working mother who has experience actually running a large governmental unit very far from Washington."[14]

It was a heady combination—you didn't get much farther away from Washington than Sarah Palin; the American people wanted change and McCain had made a bold offering to them. Moreover, as Nessen acknowledged, Palin had the real potential to reach women voters—touching them with her story, translating her experience as a woman that reflected their own life experiences into a voice at the highest level of government.

As soon as Palin hit the campaign trail, the money started rolling in. ABC News reported that the McCain campaign raised more than $10 million in the two and a half days after Palin was announced. Said one McCain campaign official, "We were blown away. . . . She has energized our base and when we see the money flowing like that we know we have a hit."[15]

But for all the praise she received for her initial performance before the American public—and for all the much-needed money that she was able to bring in—what happened next was startling to those of us who know our way around political campaigns, and it was very likely disconcerting to the public who had demonstrated such enthusiasm for the new candidate.

There was absolutely no follow-on media tour "introducing Palin" to the nation. The reasons remain unclear but there was no follow-up to Palin's thrilling beginning. There were no talk radio or cable news interviews—not even friendly ones, with sympathetic interviewers throwing soft questions. There weren't even any of those staged "roundtable" meetings with "average Americans" taped by pool reporters and broadcast across the country. Instead, it seemed that Palin went into—or was put into—hiding from the media except in highly controlled campaign events in which she took no questions. Could it be that the McCain campaign valued her more for her looks and her image than for what she might do for America?

The lack of media appearances was especially surprising because at those campaign events—out on the stump—Palin was wildly popular. She turned out record crowds rivaling Obama's in battleground states. In Tampa, Florida, she drew a crowd estimated at over twenty-five thousand, according to the *Tampa Tribune*.[16] The *Roanoke Times* estimated that even with "the wind chill approached freezing," sixteen thousand people showed up for a Palin speech in Salem, Virginia.[17] There was even anecdotal evidence to suggest that at joint McCain-Palin rallies the crowd would start to thin out after Palin spoke: folks didn't even stick around to hear McCain—they wanted Palin.

This much is clear: the McCain campaign did her no favors, and Palin was either complicit or unable to reverse it. Whatever the reason, the problem remained that the American public had been given a glimpse of someone they had immediately taken to—and then she was taken away from them. Access denied.

Into that void stepped others who would define the absent vice presidential candidate.

We've talked a bit about how Obama exploited new technologies to his advantage in the campaign; let's go a bit deeper into that subject. In a blog for CNN, I wrote in September of 2002 about how, in 1840, a young Whig organizer named Abraham Lincoln compiled a guidebook on political field work. His "confidential" circular advised Whig campaign operatives to "make a perfect list of all the voters and ascertain with certainty for whom they will vote." Almost 170 years later, Democratic presidential candidate Barack Obama was demonstrating the wisdom of Lincoln's counsel.

Computers, of course, had long since replaced the 3-by-5 cards that for generations were the stock in trade of precinct captains in both political parties—green cards for voters who supported your candidate, red ones for those opposed, and white cards for the undecided. Every campaign needed to persuade the white cards, get out the green cards on Election Day, and keep a close watch on turnout by the red cards. Marrying creative marketing techniques with state-of-the-art technology, Obama had taken the voter identification process to lengths nobody could have anticipated only four years before. What this meant was that the Obama campaign had found a way to coax out a more detailed voter profile, which it could then use to mobilize voters in critical states on Election Day. Team Obama even cleverly used e-mail and mobile texting "sign ups" so supporters could be "the first" to learn of his vice presidential selection.

But there was another—perhaps even more profound—way that this kind of database was an advantage for Obama. By collecting cell phone numbers and e-mail addresses on a scale that no campaign had done before his, Obama was in a position to stay ahead of and counter any negative news stories that might make a difference in a close race. Through e-mails, texting, or Twittering, he could immediately—and in a way that young people, especially, had come to think of as personal contact—answer any negative press about Jeremiah Wright, Bill Ayers, or any other questionable assertion that was made about him.

In the primaries, Clinton enjoyed no such networking—and it was one tool that she might have been able to exploit to her advantage: Women are among the primary users of this technology—and not just young women. While young people were early adopters of new technology, older Americans were soon to follow—with exceptions. My mom, for instance, was a fast learner, but the other day she asked me if I was "textmexing" her. My mom is not alone. Women all over America, no matter their age, are beginning to utilize social media platforms to build their own communities. I'm not sure if that's because we tend to be more social than men, or if we're just smarter when it comes to technology. The point is that we have a leg up, and across generations, on the new ways people talk to each other. This could have been used to Clinton's great benefit had she—or her campaign managers—not stuck to the old, traditional ways of campaigning. As women, we can't let the potential of social media go untapped, as it can be one of our most useful tools in building the kind of national communities a candidate needs to make a credible race for the presidency.

But, not to look too far ahead before we've studied our history, the McCain campaign was even further behind in figuring out how to employ the new technology, and Palin was the one who was most affected. There are two main reasons Palin suffered for her campaign's lack.

As John C. Abell, the New York bureau chief of Wired.com explained it:

> The main difference is the speed of the news cycle now. A generation ago it was Johnny Carson jabbing you in his *Tonight Show* monologue that raised the threat level. Because he was

topical, not political, you knew you were in trouble when Johnny started making jokes about you. Now the sum total of political commentary seems to be making jokes. You have a lot of people with access to a wide audience and the ability to recommunicate comments—"retweet," to use the correct parlance—very, very quickly. The volume and speed and access we all now have has democratized the old tastemaker dynamic.[18]

To put a really fine point on it, in the last month of the Clinton primary campaign, May 2008, with Jay Leno in Johnny Carson's old time spot, Leno joked about Clinton on twelve episodes. In the month of September 2008, just weeks before the election, Leno joked about Palin on twenty-one episodes. And those clips of Leno's jokes don't go away as they did in the Carson days.

Abell continued: "2004 was still dominated by old media and old media thinking. YouTube didn't exist yet; [nor did] the notion of viral videos and mocking and being able to 'Daily Show' somebody . . . not allowing them to reinvent what they say or had done because here's the video proof and a million people have seen it."

In sum, what this meant for Palin was, while the McCain campaign was keeping her under wraps, her story was being distorted and her family was being dissected—and usually by people who had her best interests at heart. It was here that the impact of social media on perceptions of a candidate can most easily be understood.

There is, for example, the letter written by a woman identifying herself as "a resident of Wasilla, Alaska," who had known Palin since 1992. That letter was full of damaging allegations about the way she led the city as mayor, including the charge that she had tried to fire the city librarian "because the librarian refused to consider removing from the library some books that Sarah wanted removed."[19] That letter spread like wildfire across the Internet. It was emailed and talked about and even became the focus of more than one report in the mainstream media. All this despite the fact that it included a number of factually incorrect statements including, as the Annenberg Political Fact Check.org reported, the story about Palin trying to ban books.[20]

Throughout the liberal blogosphere, on television shows that were edited in the worst possible light and then quickly became YouTube clip sensations, and—importantly—through those who were Twittering, passing along the information about these damning pieces and increasing their readership and viewership exponentially, Palin was defined by her own absence. Indeed, it got so bad that even Palin's Wikipedia entry was tampered with time and again by liberals who were set on not allowing the narrow definition with which they'd saddled her to expand in any meaningful way.

Worse in terms of how this was playing out for Palin was that, as Abell noted: "We also had a candidate in Obama who I think extraordinarily was willing to address controversial things head on for better or for worse. . . . Confronting accusations directly can be a winning strategy."

This is not to say that the McCain camp didn't tune in at all to new technologies. According to Liz Mair, the former RNC online communications director:

> I actually think a lot of the work that McCain and RNC did to engage bloggers reinforced his identity both to media, generally, and to voters, whether or not that was the point of focusing so heavily on online media outreach so far as the campaign or the RNC were concerned. In any event, though, both the RNC and the campaign did do a ton of outreach to online media—we were very aggressive in that regard. McCain himself, from very early on, did regular conference calls with bloggers—and not just conservatives either, but liberals, policy-specific folks, and others. He had bloggers on the Straight Talk Express. The Republican National Convention offered credentials to many more bloggers than did the Democratic National Convention and staff really worked to engage them in Minneapolis-St. Paul.[21]

And, as to Obama's highly touted touch with technology? Mair demurs: "I . . . frankly expected the Obama campaign to engage more with the blogosphere, and I have been told that they really did not engage as much as the RNC or the McCain campaign did at all. There was one very influential left-of-center blogger who was literally explosively angry with them by election day, and I don't believe he's the only one. I've heard complaints from others. MyBarackObama was a great tool, and Obama definitely did great and important things online during the campaign—but I think there are probably plenty of leading, left-of-center online voices who thought his communication with them was not one of the things he did well, in the least."[22]

Alas, the fact remains that Palin did not—or was not allowed to—address her critics in a timely manner. The twenty-four-hour news cycle was now a two-to-four-second "Tweet" cycle that demanded more.[23] And contemporary talk radio, the conservative counterpart to the liberal blogosphere, just couldn't keep up. Yes, Rush Limbaugh has an audience of millions—and they listen to him intently and loyally. But Limbaugh listeners tend to be both male and of an older demographic; they do not have the advantage of being connected through things like texting and Twittering that facilitate the viral spread of both accurate information and the immediate correction of information that is not accurate.

It was a grave error the McCain camp made—not using technology to refute misinformation promulgated about Palin—and it's possible that Palin may never really ever be able to recover from it. Even in 2012 those damning clips will still be retrievable on YouTube and, in case anyone's forgotten them by then, surely liberal bloggers and Twitterers and texters will take it up as their cause to remind everyone.

In 1993, Kevin Kline starred in a movie called *Dave,* playing a look-alike who winds up impersonating the president. In the movie, the real president has a stroke and is kept on life support in a restricted area of the White House by a power-mad chief of staff, played by Frank Langella. Dave fills in.

He brings in his accountant and, over bratwurst, they find $600 million to build homeless shelters for kids. At a cabinet meeting, he gets the commerce secretary to kill an expensive program to make Americans feel good about the cars they've already bought. He becomes a better, more beloved president than the real one.

Dave's tagline was, "In a country where anybody can become president, anybody just did." But the message was really that there's nothing magical about leadership, about encouraging men and women with logic and goodwill to be better than they are.

That was also the message of Sarah Palin. She's everywoman. When she takes the kids to sports practice, it's not to Washington, D.C.'s exclusive Sidwell Friends or St. Albans. Not even Fairfax or Montgomery County. She actually knows what our schools are like—and how ill-prepared our children really are for the challenges of the global marketplace. She knows how hard it is to raise children in a culture where every time they're out of your sight, they're tuning into a multibillion-dollar music, computer game, Internet and film empire that promulgates messages frequently at odds with small-town American values. She knows what it is to meet a budget—not just for a state with $11 billion in income and expenditures or for her state's seventh-biggest city, but for a family of seven. And when it comes to the central moral issues of our time, she hasn't just cast votes and given speeches. She's had to make serious life choices.

The truth is, we all know a Sarah Palin. They're the ones who organize the picnics, coach the hockey teams, run the condo association, put together the town budget and supervise the courts and the police and the highway crews, even the power grid. In fact, most of us *are* Sarah Palins, to one degree or another. But, because of the McCain camp's lack of technological prowess—coupled with what to me is still the indefensible decision not to capitalize immediately on Palin's star power—the voters may never really get to know the truth about her.

What I know to be true from listening to countless focus groups since 2004 with women, many of them swing voters, is that women continue to grow cynical and frustrated with out-of-touch politicians who fail to work together to achieve meaningful reform in health care, education, and the economy. Why, they ask, can women solve problems every day—often with people they don't necessarily agree with, like their bosses, co-workers, or relatives—but well-paid politicians can't do the same?

Cue Sarah. For me, Palin's genuine mannerisms, values, and charisma echoed the same mindset I'd been listening to for years. Palin was unapologetic in her contempt for expansive government and the need to make government accountable again. She was tough but likable, and at times refreshingly funny. I don't believe she had the chance to connect with the men and women who wanted something different—and more real. My colleagues at CNN immediately thought I'd lost my marbles—but, had I not been walking those neighborhoods for years, listening to the concerns of real men and women, I might have missed her personal connection as well.

By the time Palin did finally reappear, the stage had been set and not in her favor. The most obvious blunder of the campaign season was the decision to focus Palin on doing just a few major network interviews—first with ABC's Charles Gibson and then CBS's Katie Couric, perhaps the seminal media event of the 2008 campaign. I can't imagine what their strategic thinking was in handling what was really Palin's policy debut in this manner, but it totally backfired.

Putting aside Palin's lackluster answers—many of which were downright incoherent, as has been widely rehashed—the sit-down, long-format network interviews did not play to Palin's personal strengths. In addition, it forced Palin to be ready to address *all* issues (policy, political, and personal) in one shot. This is opposed to the usual: two minutes on the economy during a Fox News segment; a three-minute spot on taxes on conservative talk radio; a blurb during a discussion of spending and the federal debt or energy issues or whatever on CNN; a five-minute interview on children with special needs for a feature piece; a profile for *People* magazine. Why was the decision made to put pressure of that intensity on a candidate who was so new to the national scene?

The now infamous Couric interview ran over three days, between September 23 and September 25. If Palin's people agreed to spread this interview over three days, which I have to assume they did, that decision was one of the most baffling. Charitably, they must have hoped for a home run; instead, what they got was a disaster that wouldn't end. In light of Palin's poor performance in the interview, it simply ratcheted up the media attention and not in a good way. One could almost see her opponents salivating: What's she gonna say next?

Plenty of folks, including MarketWatch's Jon Friedman and CNN's Wolf Blitzer (on the air), asked why she wasn't even deployed to do the more traditional VP interviews after the presidential debates—quick and easy spots plugging John McCain's performance. As Friedman points out, instead, after the September 26 presidential debate, former "New York mayor Rudy Giuliani, who is accustomed to the media glare, pinch-hit for Palin. . . . He spoke with force, but it was anticlimactic. The nation wanted to see and hear Palin." In other words, why wasn't Sarah Palin incorporated into the media noise of the campaign—as, say, Joe Biden had been by the Obama camp?

Instead, Palin was purposely placed on the spot and in the hot seat. She had to be ready for anything and everything, and she wasn't.

What are we to believe here? Did she simply not have the chops? Was she nervous? Unpracticed? Was she so unprepared that even after being kept in a carefully media-free bubble for about twenty days she was still unable to perform well in network interviews? Did Palin herself have little choice in what she did or what she said?

Adding insult to injury, her performance was such obvious fodder for spoof. Tina Fey's masterful impression of Palin made her as much a campaign celebrity as the candidates themselves. And her Palin-isms—"I can see Russia from my house"—along with the winks and nods not only reinforced criticisms of Palin, they became synonymous with her. The *Saturday Night Live* skits practically wrote themselves—and one almost literally did. Perhaps most damningly, the *SNL* writers, rather than providing original material for Fey's skit one week, simply used Palin's own words against her. The following Sunday, split screen images of Palin's interview and Fey's near-perfect imitation of it were all over the airwaves and the Internet. Most talking heads had a good on-air, seemingly incredulous laugh at Palin's expense.

By some readings, the fallout was devastating. Looking again at Gallup's Daily Tracking Poll: between September 22 and 24, Obama and McCain had been locked in a tie, each polling at 46 percent; three days later, in a poll taken in the time period between September 25 and 27, after the Couric interview aired, Obama was up by eight points—50 percent to McCain's 42 percent.[24]

At first glance, this looks like a clear-cut case: Palin bombed and the polls followed. But the deeper truth is not so clear. First of all, these polls aren't perfect; there's a margin of error. More important, campaigns don't occur in a bubble. There was a lot going on in the nation and in the world. For one thing, *the economy was tanking*. Global markets were falling, the credit markets had seized up, and the U.S. Congress was debating a massive bailout plan that was unpopular with many Americans. And, at least politically speaking, the economic downturn clearly benefited Obama, enabling him to point not at McCain but at the Bush administration and link the candidate with the unpopular sitting president. The economic freefall bolstered Obama's case for change (even if just for the sake of change!).

What happened on September 24—not even on the heels of these enormous events but almost simultaneously with them—was McCain's disastrous, distracting decision to suspend his campaign because of the "historic crisis in our financial system." He also made a play to delay the first presidential debate, which was scheduled to occur on September 26, on the grounds that his energies would be better spent in dealing with the financial crisis than taking part in politics.

The media had a field day with that, wondering on air what McCain believed he could accomplish in Washington when by his own admission economics had never been one of his strong suits. Leading the pack was comedian David Letterman. McCain abruptly canceled a scheduled appearance on the *The Late Show with David Letterman,* claiming he was heading to Washington to resolve the economic crisis, only to be caught live on the set of *CBS Evening News* for an interview with Katie Couric. What followed was several days of relentless comedic assaults by the CBS late night hosts. Meanwhile, the video clip of McCain making this damning admission seemed to play ceaselessly, and the debate went forward anyway. This gave Obama an opening for a terrifically pejorative line: "It's going to be part of the president's job to deal with more than one thing at once."[25] All of this was going on while the still wildly popular Palin was pulled again from public view except, of course, for those big, carefully controlled rallies where she shone.

So there was plenty of blame to go around. But here's the bottom line: whatever the reasons—and it was probably a combination of all these factors, including the Couric mess—the McCain-Palin ticket never recovered. They would never again come close to leading Obama-Biden. The damage was done.

In the midst of a growing economic crisis, and in spite of the heat she was taking in the media, Palin found herself prepping for her debate with Senator Joe Biden on October 2. To say that the pressure on her to perform was high is an understatement. It was now or never, and the viewing audience for that one-and-only debate was projected to be higher than for the presidential debates.

Indeed, the Pew Research Center has reported that during the week of the vice presidential debate, it was the top election story—by a wide margin—accounting for more than half (52 percent) of that week's election coverage across all media sources. Among the candidates, Palin, in particular, dominated the coverage, "registering as a significant or dominant newsmaker in 51 percent of the campaign stories."[26]

And, let's face it: a lot of the reason for the intense focus on Palin was that the expectations for her debate performance were pretty low. Many people were tuning in just to see if Palin would fall flat on her face. As Queen Latifah—playing debate moderator Gwen Ifill on *Saturday Night Live*—would later parody: "We would like to remind our audience that due to the historically low expectations for Governor Palin, were she simply to do an adequate job tonight, and at no point cry, faint, run out of the building, or vomit, you should consider the debate a tie. [Insert Fey-Palin wink!]"[27]

There was much reporting about Palin's "debate prep" and about internal strife in the McCain camp in the week leading up to the debate. A *Wall Street Journal* story was titled "Game Plan for Palin Is Retooled Ahead of Debate: Top McCain Aides Oversee Preparation After Recent Flubs," and reported that Palin was being flown to McCain's Arizona ranch to prepare.[28]

But the senior McCain aides got the joke. They knew they had to "let Palin be Palin," as one of them put it. Another said: "People love Sarah Palin and she's got a unique personality and presence we need to bring out—not shut down."[29]

As the Pew Research Center has reported, an estimated 73 million viewers tuned in for the vice presidential debate—the second-most-watched political debate in U.S. history (behind only the 1980 Carter-Reagan match-up).[30] And, in the end, both candidates were thought to have performed relatively well. Palin's debate performance was not the disaster some had hoped for. It was good. It wasn't a home run; she made some mistakes, but it was solid.

It was also probably too late—and by that I don't mean for the McCain-Palin ticket because, as I noted a few paragraphs earlier, the bottom line is that it would have taken a miracle for them to recover after the bungle of announcing a campaign shutdown. That was such a wrong step. But it was too late, by this point, for Palin to really have a chance of retooling in the public imagination before Election Day. She had become a caricature of her winking, "mavericky" self.

The media—with special mention of *Saturday Night Live*—had played a role in this, to be sure. Indeed, as Pew reported, by the end of October, more "than half of the public (56 percent) heard *a lot* about Palin's appearance on 'Saturday Night Live.' . . . As many Americans said they heard about Palin's *SNL* appearance as said they heard about her being chosen as John McCain's running mate at the end of August."[31]

But it wasn't just the *SNL* parodies—and their viral spread online and through major media outlets. This was as much the doing of the McCain campaign and Palin herself. When we first met Palin, she was "just an average hockey mom from Alaska" and that worked well as a cutesy introductory device. But she held on to that for too long. As of September 3, 2008, she was anything but "average." She was the Republican vice presidential candidate, and she needed to pivot into that role more convincingly. By not doing so, she left herself open to criticism that was only exacerbated by her limited media exposure and her weak performance on the outlets the McCain campaign did allow to her—she's a lightweight, she's not ready, she's not smart enough, the media said, and the voters agreed.

Prominent defections from the McCain camp, including Christopher Hitchens and Christopher Buckley, used Palin as their excuse to bail from a leaky campaign boat. Those defections were just one more nail in the Republicans' collective coffin for this election cycle.

As a result, Palin's favorability ratings—initially very high—fell drastically and quickly. On September 5, 2008, Rasmussen Reports had her favorability rating among American voters at 58 percent, a point higher than either McCain or Obama enjoyed and, at the time, 10 percentage points higher than Biden's. Men viewed Palin more favorably than women did—65 percent to 52 percent.[32]

At about the same time, Gallup had Palin's favorability rating at 53 percent (with 19 percent still having no opinion or being unfamiliar with her). But by October 31, that number had fallen to 42 percent, with 49 percent viewing her unfavorably. During that same period, by contrast, Joe Biden's favorability rating moved from 49 percent to 53 percent (with his unfavorable level consistently around 30 percent).[33]

Palin more than held her own in the debate, but it wasn't good enough to stop the bleeding. The Pew Research Center's review of all media coverage from the debate concluded that the "media consensus was that both candidates had done better than expected. And the widely accepted view among pundits was that the debate was not a game changer."[34] It's fair to ask if *anything* would have been good enough for Palin—if, considering the consensus that seemed to be taking shape around her, she could have done anything that the pundits would have wholeheartedly approved of.

As the conservative commentator Ross Douthat wrote online for the *Atlantic,* Biden

> didn't need to wipe the floor with her in order to win, and he wisely didn't try; he just needed to sound more authoritative, nuanced, and experienced than her, to hammer away at John McCain, and to generally play defense for a ticket that's on its way to victory at the moment. And I think he succeeded. . . . So while Sarah Palin did an awful lot for Sarah Palin tonight, there was only so much she could do for her running mate—given her own limits, but especially given the state of the country, and the gulf between the issues the McCain campaign wants to fight on and the issues voters care about. She's saved herself from Quayledom, but Obama-Biden is one debate closer to victory.[35]

Underscoring all of the commentary on the debate were the weeks and weeks of incessant negative coverage of Palin. There was her "lack of experience" to blather about, and her "beauty queen" looks for the pundits to gnaw on, but perhaps more significantly there was the stunningly sexist scrutiny about her family, and how her responsibilities as a wife and mother would affect her performance as vice president.

A May 2008 *New York Times* article speculated that "a woman who runs for president will have to be married with children, which to voters signifies middle America. . . . But while it's an asset for men to have young children—so Jack Kennedy!—a woman with the same tends to make voters wonder who will take care of them. (That might temporarily bench Ms. Palin, who recently had her fifth child . . .)."[36]

CNN's John Roberts, a former medical correspondent, faced tremendous criticism when he said,

> We've talked about her experience and what depth of experience she has; the fact that maybe she tries to peel off a few women voters on the Democratic side, who really wanted to see a woman in the White House in some way, shape, or form. . . . There's also this issue that on April eighteenth, she gave birth to a baby with Down syndrome. . . . Children with Down syndrome require an awful lot of attention. The role of Vice President, it seems to me, would take up an awful lot of her time, and it raises the issue of how much time will she have to dedicate to her newborn child?[37]

"Looking back, I wish I hadn't brought it up," he told me. "Because it was a non-issue."

The *New York Times* ran a story examining how with "five children, including an infant with Down syndrome and, as the country learned Monday, a pregnant seventeen-year-old, Ms. Palin has set off a fierce argument among women about whether there are enough hours in the day for her to take on the vice presidency, and whether she is right to try." How does she do it all, folks? According to the *Times,* it's the "Mommy Wars: Special Campaign Edition." Among other things, the story quoted an admitted Obama supporter and mother from Oregon who opined: "You can juggle a BlackBerry and a breast pump in a lot of jobs, but not in the vice presidency."[38] The apparent truth that a woman with an infant is automatically disqualified for the vice presidency went unchallenged by the *Times.*

Some of the sexism Palin endured was cleverly couched as legitimate debate, and it boiled down to this: *she can't possibly do it all and do it well.* The obvious question is whether a man with a similarly large and young family would've gotten this same degree of scrutiny. And the simple answer is no.

As Georgetown University professor Deborah Tannen put it: "What we're dealing with now, there's nothing subtle about it . . . we're dealing with the assumption that child-rearing is the job of women and not men. Is it sexist? Yes." Hillary Clinton's former strategist Howard Wolfson agreed, saying, "There's no way those questions would be asked of a male candidate."[39] Similarly, McCain campaign strategist Steve Schmidt said, "I can't imagine that question being asked of a man. I think it's offensive, and I think a lot of women will find it offensive."[40]

But too few actually did. Not enough to make a difference at the polls, and I have to wonder why. Certainly not for the reason Schmidt implies, that women should have voted for Palin because they were outraged by the way Palin was treated by the press. If that was the plan, no wonder they lost.

Tying the question of Palin's competency to her motherhood was not where the sexism ended. To cite just a few other examples, there was the uproar over her wardrobe, including a lengthy critique of her style in the *Washington Post* titled "Sarah Palin's Unassertive Fashion Statement."[41] There was the wildly unfounded speculation that her infant son was in fact her daughter's child, and this was closely related to the near-obsession with her daughter's pregnancy and whether or not it would derail Palin's chances. There were the constant references to her as a "diva."

There was ABC reporter David Wright's comparison of then-governor Palin to a trophy wife when appearing alongside McCain: "The difference in their age sometimes making them an awkward pairing. In small groups, Palin can seem like the young, trophy running mate."[42]

And even satirist Maureen Dowd had her fun with her in a column entitled "Vice in Go-Go Boots?"

> Palinistas, as they are called, love Sarah's spunky, relentlessly quirky "Northern Exposure" story from being a Miss Alaska runner-up, and winning Miss Congeniality, to being mayor and hockey mom in Wasilla, a rural Alaskan town of 6,715, to being governor for two years to being the first woman ever to run on a national Republican ticket. (Why do men only pick women as running mates when they need a Hail Mary pass? It's a little insulting.)[43]

Insulting doesn't even begin to cover it.

Media scrutiny is not, in and of itself, sexist. Questioning Sarah Palin on her policy views and her experiences was not a prima facie example of sexism. Just as questions raised about Barack Obama's experience to lead were not racist.

What we need to look at, though, is whether Palin got different treatment because she was a woman. And the answer is clearly yes. As CNN's Candy Crowley put it: "My main complaint [with a lot of the coverage] was not that Sarah Palin was torn apart, it's that Joe Biden wasn't."

In some ways, data about Palin's media saturation supported this claim. In late October 2008, the Pew Research Center for People & the Press found that 46 percent of Americans said they'd "been hearing too much about Palin," while "very few (20 percent) say they've been hearing too much about Joe Biden." Instead, "38 percent say they have been hearing too little about Biden."[44]

Most of what they were hearing about Palin was negative. Right or left, I think we can all agree that asking if her large family and young children would impede her work as vice president was out of line. Certainly no one asked Obama, whose children are as young as Palin's, if caring for his two daughters would impede his ability to govern. But just as certainly we didn't see a strong defense of Palin's right to run without being dogged by questions about her ability to "do it all."

We didn't see it from many leading women's groups, who one might have expected to recoil on her behalf, and we didn't see it from members of the media, except possibly sporadically.

There were exceptions: ABC's Cokie Roberts comes to mind. In an August 30, 2008 article titled "ABC Anchor Impugns Sarah Palin as a Neglectful Mother," Rich Noyes told the story:

> On ABC's *Good Morning America* on Saturday, co-anchor Bill Weir bristled with hostility during an interview with a McCain campaign spokesman about the choice of Alaska Governor Sarah Palin as the Republican vice presidential candidate, suggesting she was unqualified and too conservative.

At one point, Weir even suggested that by running for Vice President, the Governor would be jeopardizing her four-month old daughter [*sic*], who has Down's Syndrome. Weir confronted McCain political director Mike DuHaime: "Adding to the brutality of a national campaign, the Palin family also has an infant with special needs. What leads you, the Senator, and the Governor to believe that one won't affect the other in the next couple of months?"

When DuHaime offered a general answer about Palin's "incredible life story," an obviously irritated Weir jumped in, exclaiming "She has an infant—she has an infant with special needs. Will that affect her campaigning?" Just a few moments later, that line of questioning was quickly criticized by ABC's Cokie Roberts as sexist. Without mentioning Weir, Roberts said questions "about who's taking care of the children . . . traditionally had very much angered women voters when women candidates are asked those questions and male candidates never are."[45]

So what does all of this mean in the end? The women and men who most strongly supported Palin were white, suburban, married, mostly from red states, and conservative evangelicals. And this didn't vary much over the course of the campaign. That was the fundamental problem. The McCain-Palin base didn't expand.

Though the Republican ticket got a large bump from women soon after the public met Palin, they didn't hold it. The gender gap persisted—with Obama winning 56 percent of women to McCain's 43 percent.[46] Nowhere was the gap wider than among unmarried women (single, separated, divorced, or widowed), a group Obama won 70 percent to 29 percent; while married women voted for McCain by a much slimmer margin—50 percent to 47 percent.[47]

As with all campaigns that fail, the reasons are many and complicated: first and foremost, there's the presidential candidate himself; there's the campaign and how it's run; there's the national mood and the issues that are at the forefront of Americans' minds. None of these factors worked for McCain. His opponent beat him at every turn.

It is also true that Sarah Palin's ascendancy, which at first looked so promising and positive, was anything but. As with

Hillary Clinton, her fall was her own campaign's doing—but it was aided and abetted by an undercurrent of sexism that just wouldn't go away, and by the too few who came to her defense.

I also believe that a lot of women learned a valuable lesson: Like me, they didn't believe that sexism was a major factor in their lives. When we lost a promotion or didn't get invited to the important meeting with the big boys, well, that was because we hadn't earned it yet. All we had to do was work harder and then we'd see the rewards. But the treatment Palin received from the press—not to mention from the women's groups one would have expected to come loudly and largely to her defense—made us realize there is something to this after all.

3

WOMEN'S GROUPS AND SARAH PALIN

IS PALIN A FEMINIST? DOES IT MATTER?

*S*ARAH PALIN IS A WOMAN who worked as hard as anybody to attain her goal—she was smart and savvy and performed like a champion at every task that was assigned to her as the GOP ticket's No. 2—and she was pilloried for it at every turn.

A lot of it was unfair. A lot of it was *ad hominum*. And a lot of it could be dismissed out of hand. But some of it was disquieting, especially the way the feminists groups I had expected to come out swinging in support of Palin—like the National Organization for Women and the Feminist Majority Foundation—not only remained silent while she was being pilloried but played an active role in undermining her as a woman as part of their effort to discredit her as a candidate. Were it not for the conservative voices of the Independent Women's Forum or Concerned Women for America, it seemed almost as if there were no women's groups speaking on her behalf.

"Take that, feminists," said Janice Shaw Crouse, director and senior fellow of Concerned Women for America's Beverly LaHaye

Institute. "Here is a woman of accomplishment who brings a fresh face to traditional values and models the type of woman most girls want to become."[1]

I remember going out for dinner during the campaign with a group of liberal women who are friends of mine. We talked about the election—no surprise there. Now, in the company of these women, self-defined feminists, I perhaps should have exercised some caution, but, because they are my friends, I felt comfortable talking about how distressing the attacks on Palin were to me as a woman.

They response I got from them shocked me. "How could you support *her?*" they asked. The assumed that, as a career woman, I would be naturally offended by certain of the governor's policy convictions.

I was dumbfounded, and I turned the question around on them. "How could you *not* support Palin?" How could it be that this woman's energy and passion and, yes, her incredible story of hard work and independence had not moved them to embrace her candidacy with the same conviction that I had?

Or, failing that—failing to "get" Palin as a candidate because she was a Republican or because my friends were what we call "single issue" voters—how was it possible that, as women, they couldn't at least defend her against the sexist attacks that were piled on her on a daily basis?

If they couldn't get behind her as a candidate, why couldn't they at the very least applaud her candidacy as a fellow woman? Didn't the "sisterhood" mean anything to them?

I was flummoxed. Then I read Myrna Blyth's September 17, 2008 "Palin Power" column for *National Review* online:

> We all know it's not Palin's take on the issues, or even her lack of experience, that is driving many women in the media crazy (especially those speechwriter Chriss Winston calls "The Sisterhood of the Traveling Rants"). What is really frightening them is that the woman who finally might do it, break through the glass ceiling, might not have "Democrat" stamped on her uterus.

She might not feel that American women, just because they are women and no matter what life hands them, are victims.

Aha! Comes the dawn!
Blyth continued:

And as for how Sarah should handle the out-to-get-her media, Candace Beuhner [a blogger] has some good advice: "Can you believe Charlie Gibson?" she writes. "He reminded me of my four-and-a-half-year-old reprimanding my three-year-old. The whole superior air, followed by an elaborate instruction in the 'right' way of doing something, with the grand finale of, 'Yes, well, that's because I'm smarter than you.' In our house, that whole tableau is usually followed by my three-year-old giving his big brother a big whomp on the head. I kept wanting [Palin] to say, 'Come off it, Charlie. We all know who you're voting for.' I just wish she could have taken him caribou hunting."

How was it possible that the women's groups were missing this patronization that Blyth's readers were picking up on? Or, more to the point, why were these women approving of—even gleeful at— another woman being so obviously belittled on the national stage? This is the question that needs to be asked.

For all the machinations about Sarah Palin's role in the 2008 presidential campaign—and the ongoing speculation about her political future—one question still lingers: Why didn't more prominent women's groups come to Sarah Palin's defense? Or, to put it more bluntly, why were some so set on her demise?

South Florida mom Tami Nantz was outraged by the mainstream media's treatment of Palin. From her home, she started her first blog, Moms4SarahPalin.net. "I simply started the blog to have a voice and defend Governor Palin," Nantz said. "I had never previously inserted myself this way into politics; it was new territory for me. I established the blog, and then sat on it for a few days. When I came back to it, I couldn't believe the traffic I'd had; I figured I was onto something."[2]

She was. As Elaine Lafferty asked on The Daily Beast: "Why do we demonize or worship certain charismatic female politicians, projecting either our most unrealistic hopes on them or our worst fears? Palin got caught in this. And the McCain campaign remained clueless, even as they watched it happen. This 'love her or hate her' business isn't good for women."[3]

That's an understatement. Lafferty has hit on a key to the problem any party will have in electing a woman to the highest office in the land, and if we don't address it head on, it's going to be a long, long time until any woman—Republican or Democrat—can overcome it.

So, what *was* it about Sarah Palin? Was it just about the issues? Was that the real objection that liberals had about Palin? After all, though Palin was an unapologetically pro-life, pro-gun candidate, women and men who disagreed with her on those and a host of other issues surely had the right to *not* vote for her—and to campaign for the candidate they did agree with. Why wasn't simply campaigning against, or voting against, Palin enough in this case? Why was it so very necessary for some people to demonize her?

Let me begin with an understatement: People certainly did campaign against Palin. And some of those were women who were well known—even iconic—in the women's movement. According to Politico.com, "a spokeswoman for the National Organization for Women, noting Palin's opposition to abortion rights and support of other parts of the social conservative agenda [said:] "She's more a conservative man than she is a woman on women's issues. Very disappointing."

NOW president Kim Gandy later disputed this comment, saying, "[I]t is inaccurate because it did not come from a spokesperson for the organization and does not reflect NOW's policy or position,"[4] but the idea that the NOW spokesman's anti-female feminist assault was an isolated incident was belied by the women's movement's biggest star, Gloria Steinem herself.

In her widely read September 7, 2008, op-ed piece on Palin in the *Los Angeles Times,* Gloria Steinem wrote:

Here's the good news: Women had become so politically powerful that even the antifeminist right wing—the folks with a headlock on the Republican party—are trying to appease the gender gap with a first-ever female vice president. We owe this to women—and to many men too—who have picketed, gone on hunger strikes or confronted violence at the polls so women can vote. We owe it to Shirley Chisholm, who first took the 'white-males-only' sign off the White House, and to Hillary Rodham Clinton, who hung in there through ridicule and misogyny to win eighteen million votes. But here is even better news: It won't work. This isn't the first time a boss has picked an unqualified woman just because she agrees with him and opposes everything most other women need and want. Feminism has never been about getting a job for one woman. It's about making life more fair for women everywhere.

Right. Except, that is, for women who don't follow the established feminist party line. Except for women like Palin who, Steinem added, "shares nothing but a chromosome with Clinton."[5]

As I read that, it means, "You can run, Sarah Palin, but you won't get my support because you don't believe in all the same things I believe in." It means "I'm smarter than you are, Sarah Palin." It's comments like that that prove beyond a shadow of a doubt that Sarah Palin needed the women's movement like a fish needs a bicycle.

Dee Dee Myers, whom I personally admire, in her column of August 29, 2008, "Sarah Palin: A Sleight of Gender" for the Huffington Post, was kinder—ostensibly: "What I know of Palin (which admittedly isn't much), I kind of like. I don't agree with her politics. But in her two years in Alaska's state house, she's shown herself to be a scrappy reformer, a no-nonsense manager, and a consistent conservative. She's also a mother of five, which in my book is a sterling test of leadership."

Nice stuff, right? Palin is a competent, qualified candidate. Wait for it . . . here it comes . . . the big *but she's not really qualified*:

Clearly, McCain thinks Palin will help him among women, particularly those disaffected Hillary Clinton supporters who are having so much trouble "getting over it." It just shows how clueless the McCain camp actually is. Unlike Clinton and Ferraro, Palin hasn't been a strong national voice on women's issues. She hasn't been at the barricades, fighting for women's health, equal pay, economic security. And she certainly hasn't had anything to say about the national security issues that are also important to women across the political spectrum. Does the McCain camp really expect pro-choice Democratic and independent women to be swayed by a sleight-of-gender?[6]

It gets worse—Myers actually assumed that Palin would fail. And, in that case, the woman from whom she withheld her support would make all women look bad: "when Palin falls short . . . some people will conclude that women can't cut it."

The pressure heaped upon Palin's slim shoulders would have broken someone of a lesser spirit, yet break her spirit is exactly what these women intended to do. While Myers, as I said, was kinder than most of Palin's critics, some of Myers's readers responded to her column in the Huffington Post with a total lack of compassion—and decency.

With reference to Myers's defense of Palin's decision-making skills, one reader posted this stinging rebuke:

> What kind of judgment does it display that [Palin] chose to have more children in her mid-40's? The likelihood of having birth defects and other problems increases by a lot as one gets older and past the "normal" child bearing years. Even from the husband's side. And if what I heard is true that she wants more children, what does that say about her judgment? Downs Syndrome is a genetic disease so either she or her husband or both carry this gene. If having a working uterus is the main qualification for women Veeps, then most women qualify. I would like to think that most women know how to manage their uterus much better than she has done.[7]

The attacks on Palin were not based on policy differences, they were personal. And they were very, very ugly.

Lafferty, a Democrat, an avowed feminist and former editor of *Ms.* magazine (who, I'll note again for the sake of complete disclosure, also supported the McCain-Palin ticket), was one of the few traditional feminists to strongly defend both Palin's intelligence and her right to run—and to call out others for not doing the same. In Lafferty's view, "for the sin of being a Christian personally opposed to abortion, Palin is being pilloried by the inside-the-Beltway Democrat feminist establishment. . . . Bottom line: you are not a feminist until *we* say you are. And there you have the formula for diminishing what was once a great and important mass social change movement to an exclusionary club that rejects women who sincerely want to join and, God forbid, grow to lead."[8]

Why exactly was this? After all, Palin was a self-described feminist. When asked by Katie Couric if she considered herself a feminist, Palin said, "I do. . . . I'm a feminist who believes in equal rights and I believe that women certainly today have every opportunity that a man has to succeed, and to try to do it all, anyway."[9] Yes, later Palin did walk away from the "label" of feminist, but wasn't it more important that she embodied the concept of an empowered woman? Wasn't that the whole goal of the women's movement in the first place, to empower women?

As Palin said in her convention speech, "among the many things I owe [my parents] is one simple lesson: that this is America, and every woman can walk through every door of opportunity."[10] Well, Palin found herself on the threshold of the doorway to power only to find herself blocked by the very same people who should have been standing off to the side cheering.

That didn't stop her from trying to reach out for the women's vote—not to traditional feminists, but to hard-working, conservative mothers just like her. On the campaign trail, she made a pitch to women voters in Nevada on October 21, saying among other things: "Our opponents think that they have the women's vote all locked up, which is a little presumptuous . . . since only our side has a woman on the ticket. . . . You've got to ask yourself, why was Senator Hillary Clinton not even vetted by the Obama campaign? Why did it take twenty-four years, an entire generation, from the time Geraldine Ferraro made her pioneering bid, until the next time that a woman was asked to join a national ticket?"[11]

Incredibly, it was Palin who stood up for the feminists. She told the *Chicago Tribune*:

> I think Hillary Clinton was held to a different standard in her primary race.... Do you remember the conversations that took place about her, saying superficial things that they don't talk about with men, her wardrobe and her hairstyles, all of that? That's a bit of that double standard.... I'm not going to complain about it, I'm not going to whine about it, I'm going to plow through that, because we are embarking on something greater than that, than allowing that double standard to adversely affect us.[12]

Some in the media picked up on this trend in Palin's public comments. National Public Radio ran a piece called "Sarah Palin: New Face of Feminism?" in which Stanford University historian Estelle Freedman discussed the history of feminism and the possible emergence of a "conservative" feminism.

Freedman said, among other things, that "Democrats and Republicans are both sounding very much like would-be feminists."[13] The *Wall Street Journal* ran an opinion piece called "Sarah Palin Feminism," which focused on evangelical women and whether or not they would "stick with their woman."[14] The conservative radio talk show host Laura Ingraham argued that "Sarah Palin represents a new feminism.... And there is no bigger threat to the elites in this country than a woman who lives her conservative convictions."[15]

And, make no mistake about it, there are conservative feminists. Here's what one prominent one, April-Liesel Binapri, founder of the Feminist Alliance of Conservatives for Equality said to me about her movement:

> I wanted to "take" the feminist movement away from the liberals. I wanted to create a brand that's more formidable than NOW [National Organization for Women]. So I had to think of something and I came up with FACE for Women. Then I had to figure out what FACE stood for. And Feminist Alliance of Con-

servatives for Equality came to mind. Then FACE for Women was born. Then I wanted to snatch up a web address—www .FACEforWomen.com—and I bought it.

Look, I'm a Sarah Palin-Ronald Reagan conservative. In a dream I'd like any and all conservatives who consider themselves feminists to come together and create a sort of consensus on what "the conservative feminist agenda" is. I want to promote that as well as women candidates. I feel personally that Sarah Palin is the perfect role model for anti-establishment conservative feminists. I feel the need as a conservative feminist to make sure Sarah Palin succeeds.[16]

The bottom line is that one doesn't have to be liberal to care about women's issues. No one's got a lock on concern for women's liberty. Sandra Day O'Connor summed this up very neatly in a interview with the *New York Times* in 2009 when she responded to the question, "Do you call yourself a feminist?" with this wise answer: "I never did. I care very much about women and their progress. I didn't go march in the streets, but when I was in the Arizona Legislature, one of the things I did was to examine every single statute in the state of Arizona to pick out the ones that discriminated against women and get them changed."

No marching in the street. No bra burning. No belting out Helen Reddy. Just calm concern for how women were faring in the world—and consistent action to better their ability to lead their lives.

Many on the liberal blogosphere, not surprisingly, were none too happy that Sarah Palin was being touted as a feminist. Indeed, it seemed to strike a chord of real fear. Wrote one blogger ("Jessica") on Feministing.com, "Note to mainstream media: Sarah Palin is NOT a feminist."[17] And, perhaps predictably (in part because she was literally on the payroll of McCain-Palin), Lafferty was pounded for her comments defending Palin, including by one blogger ("Megan") on Jezebel.com who posted a lengthy entry entitled "Elaine Lafferty Is Stupid: As far as I'm concerned, former Ms. Editor Elaine Lafferty can go f*ck herself":

Meagan wrote,

Normally, I would write this post as a letter to the person I think is a complete idiot, but I've decided to toss the conceit today because I don't *want* to be on good terms with Elaine Lafferty, the former editor of *Ms.* who left under shady circumstance in 2005 that no one wants to discuss, sat on the stage with other feminists and former Clinton supporters—like Lady Lynn Forester de Rothschild—at a Palin rally last week and, despite boos from her new political compatriots every time Clinton was mentioned, continues to support the Republican ticket. In fact, in a Daily Beast column yesterday, she outed herself as a full-fledged Palin advisor and has some "wisdom" to lay on us feminists. And by wisdom, I mean a load of the most uninformed horseshit I've read this week, at least, and I read the *National Review*.[18]

A blogger (Holly) on a site called Menstrualpoetry.com had this to say: "I woke up yesterday and by the time I was awake for eleven minutes I felt like I had been punched in the gut several times after reading on several conservative blogs how Sarah Palin, McCain's VP pick, is such a great feminist role model."[19]

There was, strangely, also this entry, from Olivia St. John on September 2, 2008, titled "Sarah Palin's feminist folly":

Bristol Palin, the seventeen year old, unmarried daughter of Sarah Palin, is pregnant. Although she plans to keep the baby and marry the father, her immoral shortcoming is still clear for the nation (and world) to see. Is it possible that her very busy, avowedly-feminist mother, the governor of Alaska and presumptive Republican vice presidential candidate, could have made a moral difference, had she been more available to her daughter? With this in mind, it is sobering that, among the thousands of conservative pundits praising John McCain's selection of Sarah Palin as his vice presidential running mate, no one is asking the very important question: Does America really need a feminist in the White House?[20]

Meow. It was your typical convoluted cat fight, waged in the blogosphere.

Even if we can't agree that Sarah Palin is a feminist, at least we can agree that she was a woman who was under attack—or, at the very least, her family and her choices were undeniably under siege. And that's where the real breakdown seemed to be. Laying aside for just one rational moment any disagreement on the issues (or even about her inexperience), I'm asking why women leaders did not speak out—loudly and frequently—about the sexist treatment Palin was receiving and the undue scrutiny to which her children, in particular, were subjected. Was there really no one who had the compassion to defend her against the false rumor that her infant son, Trig, was really her daughter Bristol's child? Or to feel outrage at the fixation on Bristol's actual pregnancy when it was announced?

As Politico.com reported, "Democrats, especially on blogs and in private conversations, have savaged Palin for the news that her seventeen-year-old unwed daughter Bristol is pregnant and plans to marry the father. Liberal radio host Ed Schultz, who had already used the words 'bimbo alert' to refer to Palin, suggested that she was a hypocrite for having a pregnant child while touting a social conservative platform."[21]

By September 1, 2008, NBC's Katie Primm and Mark Murray had made a point of ferreting out an old Eagle Forum Alaska questionnaire from 2006 which asked the question: "Will you support funding for abstinence-until-marriage education instead of for explicit sex-education programs, school-based clinics, and the distribution of contraceptives in schools?" Palin had responded, "Yes, the explicit sex-ed programs will not find my support." As if a politician's earnest pledge gave them leave to mock a teenager's struggle and a family's pain.

Some in the blogosphere—even on the left—did not follow this trend (and indeed blogged against it), as for example, the Tennessee Guerilla Women: "A woman enters the presidential race and suddenly the progressive mission is to shame and mortify Sarah Palin, her children, her husband, and every woman who has ever found herself in a similar situation."[22]

This story reared its ugly head again months after the election, when Bristol Palin and her child's father announced they would not, in fact, get married, prompting renewed focus from the mainstream media and the blogosphere—a focus that had the sort of "ha, ha, I told you so" tone of revenge.

"A source says Bristol broke up with the teenage sperm donor Levi 'Sex on Skates' Johnston two months ago, won't even let him see the fruit of his loins, and has denounced the entire Johnston family as 'white trash.' . . . Really, Bristol: What do you expect people to call a girl who gets herself knocked up by white trash? This does not reflect favorably on you." This from a site that called itself "The Other McCain." But upon whom were these people seeking revenge? An adolescent girl with a tough row to hoe ahead of her? Or her mother, who dared to run for office while her daughter was gestating? There was even a Twitter bickering battle about it, for heaven's sake.

Again and again, throughout the election season, we were told—or it was implied—that Sarah Palin was unfit for the vice presidency because her teenage daughter was pregnant out of wedlock, or she was a mother of five children, or that one of her children had special needs that might distract from her ability to be vice president, I suppose by acting up at some overseas state funeral.

Liz Hunt of the *Daily Telegraph*, while claiming to be "in awe of Governor Palin's achievements, her energy, drive, ambition and commitment" also asked "just how good a 'mom' can she be, given the demands that are being made on her and the demands she is making of herself? . . . How can she reconcile such a high-profile job as 'veep'—a 'heartbeat' away from leadership of the free world and all that—with bringing up five children, the oldest of whom is about to serve in Iraq and the youngest of whom is just five months old and has Down's Syndrome?"[23]

Giving credit where credit is due, Gloria Steinem, in her widely read op-ed in the *Los Angeles Times* that ripped into comparisons between Clinton and Palin, did try to come to Palin's defense on this one point, though tepidly: "This is not to beat up on Palin. I defend her right to be wrong, even on issues that matter most to me. I regret that people say she can't do the job because she has children in need of care, especially if they wouldn't say the same about a father."[24]

Like Steinem, I didn't realize that a woman's choice to have children automatically disqualified her for the presidency, while a man is similarly unburdened. Or, at least as unburdened as an older woman whose children are grown, as are House Speaker—and second in line of presidential succession—Nancy Pelosi's five children. But if the difference, again, is that Pelosi's children are grown—and in a political system that weren't rife with sexism—wouldn't that disqualify men with young children? Barack Obama comes to mind as does John F. Kennedy or, for that matter, Jimmy Carter or Teddy Roosevelt. And, yet, from the women's groups who might have stood up with the credibility they have acquired from decades of fighting for women's rights, these sorts of obvious comparisons were never brought up.

I can only suspect that, if Hillary had been the Clinton who was running for president when Chelsea was only twelve years old, those same women's groups would have had *her* back.

We can't forget, in the litany of sexist abuses Palin suffered during the campaign, about the inane focus on her appearance and her wardrobe. The American Enterprise Institute's Norm Ornstein told *U.S. News & World Report* that "Palin gets his vote, at least in one respect. 'Sarah Palin's choice did electrify the country. . . . And I believe she's the prettiest vice presidential choice since John Edwards.'"

Commenting on Palin's slippage in favorability ratings after an initial bounce, Ornstein said, "It's just like when somebody wins *American Idol*. There's very strong interest in that person for a while, then that fades."[25] Here Palin is reduced to a pretty pop flash in the pan—the vice presidential candidate as Carrie Underwood. Is there stronger evidence that Palin just could not get the press to take her seriously?

And, of course, no list of Palin slights would be complete without mention of the campaign wardrobe the Republican National Committee purchased for her to use during the election season. "Palin Clothes Spending Has Dems Salivating, Republicans Disgusted" was the headline for a post by Sam Stein on the Huffington Post on October 22, 2008, and it was accompanied by a slide show of her stump outfits—including a photo of two adolescent boys looking up dreamily upon a stage at the VP candidate that was *shot through Palin's legs!*

Palin was even skewered for her wedding ring! From the *Christian Science Monitor,* there was this article, "Palin Wardrobe Controversy Heightens—Todd Is a Cheapo!" from October 26, 2008:

> No one is calling Todd Palin cheap or anything, but Todd . . . 35 bucks for a wedding ring? Sarah Palin threw her husband under the bus today and emboldened cheap husbands and boyfriends everywhere by announcing her wedding ring cost $35. Note that there are no commas in that figure. Those two numbers stand together. A three followed by a five. Then a period. 35 bucks. On top of this, she announced that Todd didn't even buy it. She bought it herself. Maybe this is why the *Anchorage Daily News* endorsed Barack Obama today.

The article was accompanied by a cartoon caricature of Palin fielding questions from reporters:

> Palin: I just want to talk directly to Joe Six-Pack here. Joe, the clothing thing has been blown out of proportion! It's not like I get to keep all that stuff!
> Reporter: What about the haircut?
> Palin: No, I'm giving that back too.

U.S. News & World Report's Bonnie Erbe, who is also a friend, suggested that perhaps the "strain" that some journalists claimed was emerging between McCain and Palin late in the campaign was due to, of all things, Palin's skirt length. Opined Erbe, "I didn't sense personal strain so much as generational strain. Call this an unfair generalization, but many men of McCain's generation would have a hard time being in the same room as a woman with her skirt hiked up to mid-thigh-length, much less sitting right next to her."[26]

Yes, I think I *will* call that an unfair generalization. But I'm not sure whom that's more insulting to—McCain or Palin.

The focus on Palin's wardrobe appeared to be particularly unpopular with women. In a poll commissioned by Lifetime Networks after the election, "seventy-nine percent of women said that there was too much coverage of Sarah Palin's clothing" and "64 percent of women thought the coverage of Palin was more negative than that of other candidates running for office."[27]

To be fair, some in the media did defend Palin, even if sparingly. CNN's Campbell Brown called the focus on Palin's wardrobe "an incredible double-standard," pointing out that "women are judged based on their appearance far, far more than men." Brown called the $150,000 wardrobe issue "peripheral" and challenged the media to "keep the focus on what really matters."[28] Of course, this was the same Campbell Brown that took a McCain-Palin spokesman to task on air over the way in which her leadership of the Alaska National Guard qualified her to be the U.S. commander in chief.

ABC's Cokie Roberts, in response to a question asking if women would be more likely to vote for a woman, pointed out: "That's correct, that women do not necessarily vote for women. However, if you get a lot of questions about who's taking care of the children, it might make people angry enough to vote for her, because that is something that traditionally has very much angered women voters when women candidates are asked those questions and *male candidates never are*" (emphasis added).[29]

Sadly, apparently not enough women were truly aware of how demeaning this was to Palin—at least not enough of them to get angry and stand in solidarity and vote her into office.

On a final note, and again giving credit where it is due, Hillary Clinton reportedly made it clear that she would not attack Sarah Palin personally on the campaign trail while she stumped for Obama. Said her former strategist Howard Wolfson about the "obsession in our popular culture with the 'cat fight.' . . . Editors and news executives are convinced that two women fighting sells magazines and attracts eyeballs. You can imagine the thinking: if Angelina Jolie versus Jennifer Aniston and Britney Spears versus Christina Aguilera sell copies, what could be better than Hillary Clinton v. Sarah Palin? Don't hold your breath. It's not going to happen."[30]

These defenses, particularly from the left, were generally lukewarm and all too infrequent. And so, perhaps ironically, the defense of Sarah Palin's right to run for office—even as a mother of five, egads!—fell to the right. When Phyllis Schlafly is your key defense feminist witness, you know you're locked in a partisan battle—and it's not looking good. Schlafly told the *New York Times* that having children "changes your life and gives you a different perspective on the world. . . . People who don't have children or who have only one or two are kind of overwhelmed at the notion of five children. . . . I think a hard-working, well-organized C.E.O. type can handle it very well."[31]

When conservative bloggers and radio hosts came to her defense, they didn't do Palin many favors either. Said conservative radio host Jim Quinn, "I suppose some of the hate boils down to the fact that the governor is so easy on the eyes? Hmm? That's right. See, Palin is good-looking and that drives most of these feminists, who look a lot more like Ruth Bader Ginsburg than Palin, nuts."[32]

Quinn's comment played right into what I have said was the right's initial failing in introducing Palin to the electorate: you don't tout your candidate as a "babe" and expect her to be taken seriously—apparently even by your own party's commentators.

Some analysts believed the fissure was one of a purely conservative versus liberal bias. Ben Shapiro wrote on Real Clear Politics, "The Democrats' support of women's rights, it seems, is restricted only to the most convenient political situation: liberal women versus white males. When it's liberal women versus black males—see Clinton versus Obama—the left dumps women's rights in favor of racial gains. When it's conservative women versus anybody, the left ignores women's rights completely."[33]

Representative Tom Cole of Oklahoma, then chairman of the National Republican Congressional Committee, agreed with this line of argument. Historically, Cole told Politico.com, "to be a leader in the women's movement, you have to be a liberal. This is clearly a very liberated woman who is not a liberal. And I think there is some tension with that because again, she breaks a lot of stereotypes and molds."[34]

Perhaps Camille Paglia put it most succinctly and colorfully on Salon.com:

> A feminism that cannot admire the bravura under high pressure of the first woman governor of a frontier state isn't worth a warm bucket of spit. . . . [Palin is] a world away from the whining, sniping, wearily ironic mode of the establishment feminism represented by Gloria Steinem, a Hillary Clinton supporter whose shameless Democratic partisanship over the past four decades has severely limited American feminism and not allowed it to become the big tent it can and should be. . . . Feminism, which should be about equal rights and equal opportunity, should not be a closed club requiring an ideological litmus test for membership.[35]

To me, the silence we heard from feminists about the treatment Palin and her family received was eerily reminiscent of the women's movement's reaction to the Monica Lewinsky scandal. Then, as with Palin, it was quite *inconvenient* to speak up—particularly in an election year, egads!—about the sexist, degrading (and possibly criminal) behavior of a president who, in their eyes, had done so much for women's rights.

As Christie Todd Whitman, then the Republican governor of New Jersey and very much a feminist in the traditional sense, put it in a speech at Harvard in 1998:

> Most feminist leaders have stood by and watched as women who've charged the President with improper behavior have their pasts investigated, their physical appearances ridiculed, and their lifestyles demeaned. . . . Sadly, by remaining silent, feminist leaders are sending the message that issues like gender discrimination and sexual harassment aren't always absolutely wrong. They're

only sometimes-kinda-mostly-sort of-important. . . . If you vote the right way, or appoint enough women to top positions, or advocate women-friendly policies, we can overlook your personal behavior . . . and women can't afford to have the important message of gender equality watered down by hypocrisy.[36]

In the case of Palin, it was a bit of the opposite: if you *don't* support the "right" policies, you forfeit your right to our indignation—no matter the treatment you receive.

Others saw it somewhat differently. As CNN's Candy Crowley, who covered the 2008 presidential campaigns, told me, "What some women reacted to [with Palin] was the commonality of the female experience—we've all worked hard, and we all know women who got ahead but didn't deserve it . . . she got lucky; she jumped the line."[37]

Steinem essentially echoed this sentiment, writing in her op-ed, if you'll allow me to repeat this important line: "This isn't the first time a boss has picked an unqualified woman just because she agrees with him and opposes everything most other women want and need."[38]

Given all she has done in her career to fight for women's rights and promote equal opportunity (and even in the context of this op-ed), this one sentence from Steinem is hard to swallow. It assumes, of course, that Sarah Palin does not (she could *not possibly!*) really hold the policy views and convictions she espouses. It intimates she's getting ahead by playing the boys' game—because she knows she can't hack it on her own.

In Steinem's view—and one in which she was unfortunately not alone—Palin's own issue positions and beliefs are so heretical to the rights of women that they simply *cannot* be for real. They are *only* politically expedient. This points to a fundamental problem, as Paglia and others have discussed—namely, that the feminist movement has become, more than a movement for change and the promotion of opportunity and fair treatment for all, a collection of policy stances to which all members must dogmatically conform. And to me, this doesn't feel right.

Or perhaps David Kahane got it right with his tongue-in-cheek column "I Hate You Sarah Palin," in which he wrote:

> After we sent Bill n' Hill packing with their twin gold watches in Denver, we thought we had a clear playing field . . . piece of cake, walk on the beach, a Renaissance Weekend in a non-denominational heaven for atheists. Until Sarah Marshall Palin showed up, bringing with her ten million bucks for the bad guys in three days. . . . So that's why we hate you, Sarah Marshall Palin. We hate you because you remind the other side of their wives, their girlfriends, their daughters, and make them want to fight for you against our sneers and our smears. . . . We hate you because you're smart and beautiful and we wish we had women like you on our side.[39]

As Candy Crowley said to me—and I think this sums up the last few pages quite nicely: "It was so like high school. Condescending." Amen.

Nevertheless, Palin's resignation as governor opened the door for more criticism. It was poorly handled and left most Americans with doubts about her ability and rationale. She has served to give powerful ammunition to her adversaries. And the videotape of her Wasilla news conference will never vanish—it will always be there to haunt her.

For her female supporters, this act was especially frustrating. To many, she's a quitter. Yes, staying in the governorship made her a lightning rod for continued ethics complaints. Yes, it would be difficult, if not impossible, to develop the national network she would need to run for future office in the "lower 48" from Wasilla. And there were at least a dozen other reasons, including her desire to protect her youngest child, Trig, from the media's scorn as well as to serve a "higher calling," which made resigning a calculated risk worth taking.

But none of that came across in her disastrous withdrawal from public office. To some extent, she gave a black eye to politically invested women of every stripe because it made it look as if she couldn't handle the pressure of being in the spotlight or the hard work of governing a state.

The bottom line is this: It's an open question as to whether or not it's advisable—or even acceptable—to defend someone's right to run even if you disagree with her on the issues. The answer is and must be a resounding yes. If it's not acceptable to lob these bombs at Barack Obama (and it's not) or Hillary Clinton (and it's not), then it's not acceptable to do the same to Sarah Palin.

4

WHAT IT TAKES

STEEL MAGNOLIAS

THE FIRST WOMAN to run for president was Victoria Claflin Woodhull—in 1872, almost fifty years before the passage of the Nineteenth Amendment to the U.S. Constitution gave women the right to vote. She was a wealthy newspaper owner, known nationally as the first woman to open a stock brokerage firm on Wall Street. She was nominated for president of the United States by the Equal Rights Party, a coalition of women's rights advocates and labor organizations.

Woodhull's campaign received a great deal of coverage in the media of the day—and though her candidacy did win for women the right to address Congress (which Woodhull, in 1871, became the first woman to do)—she was taken with so little gravity that historians still debate whether she actually received any votes on Election Day at all. She certainly didn't get her own—because she couldn't vote.

In 1884 Belva Ann Lockwood ran for president, also as the candidate of the Equal Rights Party. Lockwood, the first woman to argue a case before the Supreme Court of the United States, not only made the ballot, she actually won votes from the still all-male electorate. Since Lockwood's candidacy, other women have sought the presidency or served as running mates on behalf of third parties, including the communist Socialist Workers Party.

The first woman to make a bid for the White House from a major political party was Senator Margaret Chase Smith (R-ME). She briefly entered the contest for the GOP nomination in 1964. As a Republican, I take some pride in its being a woman from the GOP who made the first serious effort to break the presidential glass ceiling in the era after women won the right to vote. Smith won 224,970 votes—or nearly 4 percent of all votes cast—in 1964 in the five primaries in which she ran. Even more incredibly for the times, she finished second among eight candidates in the Illinois primary. Some people, particularly in the Midwest, were ready for a woman president over forty years ago.

As a side note, I might mention that the GOP continued to lead the way when, in 1972, Anne Armstrong of Texas became the first woman to give the keynote speech for either party at the Republican National Convention. Also—and this might surprise you—the Equal Rights Amendment (ERA) that has been one of the driving causes of the established women's liberation movement? That bill was first introduced into Congress in 1923 by Senator Charles Curtis and Representative Daniel R. Anthony—both Republicans. (Representative Anthony, as it happened, was the nephew of the suffragette Susan B. Anthony.)

One hundred years after Woodhull threw her bonnet in the ring, in 1972, Representative Shirley Chisholm (D-NY) became the first black woman to run for president. And, like Smith had done eight years before, Chisholm concentrated her campaign efforts in those states where she had the best chance of winning, focusing on those with large populations of African Americans, women's rights advocates, and liberals.

Even though she started her effort with just $44,000, her strategy paid off handsomely when she won the New Jersey primary with 67 percent of the vote. By the time the Democrats rolled into Miami for their national convention, Chisholm had 152 delegates pledged to her on the first ballot, not enough to win the nomination but more than enough to guarantee her influence within the convention's deliberations. An unprecedented showing for an unprecedented candidate.

After Chisholm's phenomenal showing it took twelve years for another woman to make such a major crack in the glass ceiling. It was not until 1984, when former vice president Walter Mondale chose New York representative Geraldine Ferraro as his running mate, that a woman actually took a place on a major party's national presidential ticket. It was a historic ticket, and Ferraro was supposed to help the Democrats exploit the so-called "gender gap" with support from the National Organization for Women and other women's groups by portraying President Ronald Reagan as "a sinister foe to women." M. Stanton Evan's piece from the September 16, 1988 issue of *National Review* explains that despite these efforts, Reagan "carried the women's vote by a majority of 55 to 45 percent" and that "conservative women outnumbered liberals by 33 to 24 percent."[1] What they neglected to realize was that as much as women may not have liked Reagan, white men disliked Mondale by even wider margins, and the Republicans gave the Democrats their worst Electoral College drubbing in the history of the Republic.

After Ferraro, Colorado Democrat Patricia Schroeder and North Carolina Republican Elizabeth Dole both entered the primary field. Neither lasted long. Schroeder was urged by supporters to run after frontrunner Gary Hart's campaign collapsed, but she decided ultimately that it was too late in the primary season for her to raise the money to compete reasonably with the seven male Democrats who had already been campaigning for months.

Dole, who headed both the U.S. Departments of Transportation and Education and is married to the former GOP Senate majority leader and 1996 presidential nominee Bob Dole, had earned a lot of good will campaigning for Republicans all over America.

But she too folded her campaign for lack of funds and threw the momentum she'd generated, and her ever-increasing political capital, into a winning run for a seat in the U.S. Senate.

In 1992, Democrat Carol Moseley Braun became the first African American woman to be elected to the U.S. Senate after she ousted the incumbent Democrat, the venerable Alan Dixon, in the party primary. The outcome of the general election was a foregone conclusion since Moseley Braun rode on a wave of anti-incumbent sentiment and benefited from the support of an "army of angry women voters"[2] disappointed with Senator Dixon's vote for the confirmation of Clarence Thomas to the Supreme Court. By 2004, having been voted out of office after a single term, Moseley Braun also made a run for president, getting her name on more presidential primary ballots than *any* other major party candidate in the history of the country.

Clearly, new pathways toward political power for women have developed since Woodhull's first venture onto the national stage through the suffrage movement. In the early twentieth century, most women entered public service with a "widow's mandate" of providing "a seamless transition by carrying forward the legislative business and district interests of their deceased husbands."[3] Similarly, other women have benefited from their own family's (generally the father's) political career as a launch pad for public office in solidifying their credentials. Current examples include Senators Mary Landrieu (D-LA) and Lisa Murkowski (R-AK). There is also a new emerging category of "cause chicks" motivated by a desire to impact their local communities and beyond, such as Washington senator Patty Murray's roots as a "mom in tennis shoes"[4] fighting education cuts. Whatever their background, however, women continue to change the dynamics of American politics.

What have we learned from these women pioneers? What have we learned, in particular, from our latest election? What do the 2008 candidacies of Hillary Rodham Clinton and Sarah Palin tell us about the role of women in U.S. politics going forward? What do we know, and what can other candidates—women, and men as well—learn from their experiences?

Let's start with the obvious, largely positive conclusions. First, Clinton and Palin both proved that women can meet the all-important money test. If you can't raise money, you can't win elections. Hillary Clinton pulled in more than $100 million for her presidential bid. It wasn't enough, particularly in light of her opponent's spectacular ability to raise funds on the Internet, but it's still a heck of a lot of money for a campaign that didn't produce the eventual nominee. It surpasses Chisholm's $44,000 which, even adjusted for inflation, is less than a quarter of a million dollars.

Sarah Palin's ability to raise funds was equally staggering—especially to Democrats—and immediate. Keep in mind that until McCain officially accepted the Republican nomination—and thus switched to public financing—he could still raise money. McCain-Palin "raised $9 million in the three days following his August twenty-ninth selection of Alaska governor Sarah Palin as his running mate, according to Federal Election Commission records."[5]

According to NBC News, in just one eleven-hour period, between 1:00 p.m. and midnight on the day Palin's selection was announced, the McCain campaign brought in $4.5 million.[6] Once the general election started, in fact, Palin was the primary fundraiser for the RNC and congressional candidates, and her success in this arena was outstanding. The old question of whether or not a female candidate could raise the kind of money needed to mount a serious national presidential campaign has been answered: she can.

Beyond the fact that they could competitively finance a national campaign, what else did they prove?

Both Clinton and Palin energized their base of support and drew thousands to their rallies. The emotional connection their supporters made to each candidate was extraordinary. Clinton's supporters were so stalwart that their loyalty to the candidate threatened to derail the Democratic convention when their candidate lost and, even though the derailment never happened *formally*, some of her supporters were so faithful they refused to fall in with the party line and formed rebel factions like "Party Unity My Ass," or "PUMAs," as they came to be known.

And, as previously discussed, Palin's convention speech electrified Republicans, especially conservatives, and the size of her rallies rivaled Obama's in key battleground states like Florida and Virginia.

But, perhaps most significant for future women candidates, Clinton and Palin proved that the United States is ready for a woman president or vice president.

The polls had been showing for years that a majority of Americans said they would vote for a qualified woman candidate for president from their own political party. But in 2006, a CBS News–*New York Times* poll found that the number of adults who now said they would vote for a woman for president from their own political party had risen to 92 percent. This was, actually, a pretty dramatic shift from earlier polls. In 1955, Gallup conducted a poll that showed only 52 percent would vote for a woman for president. In 1975, that number rose to 73 percent and, in 1987, it had risen to 82 percent.[7]

But there is another side of the question: in 2006, while 92 percent of Americans said they, personally, would vote for a woman, only 55 percent thought the country was ready for a woman president. Thirty-eight percent said the country just wasn't there yet.

Further, among respondents who said the country was ready, most of them were men. Sixty percent of men, compared to 51 percent of women, gave the thumbs up to a woman chief executive. Young people were also more likely to say that Americans were ready for a woman president than were older voters.

Seniors were fairly evenly split on the question, with 46 percent saying the nation wasn't ready to 44 percent who said it was. For the record, we ought to acknowledge one more outcome of that poll: Democrats were more likely to think a woman could win a presidential election than were Republicans. Sixty-one percent of respondents who identified themselves as "liberal" said a woman could be president, compared to 48 percent of respondents who identified themselves as "conservative" or "moderate." Within just two years of that poll, however, Hillary Clinton received on the order of 18 million votes. She proved that she had the national appeal it takes for any candidate, man or woman, to win. She won in traditionally liberal states—like California and Massachusetts—as well as in traditionally swing states, like Ohio and Pennsylvania, from a base of support that consisted of three core groups: low-income whites, Hispanics, and women.[8]

As important as any other gain to emerge from the 2008 campaign, Clinton effectively put to rest any claims about a man's being perceived as inherently more qualified to be commander in chief. She led her primary opponent on the "experience to lead" question throughout the campaign and on questions about her ability to command our troops. Ironically, it was Clinton's excessive focus on the experience factor—at the expense of other qualities of leadership and any claims to being able to bring about change—that probably hurt her.

That last observation is key. During the 2008 election, America was a nation fighting wars on two fronts. Given historical voting patterns in times of war and in times of peace, it was perfectly natural to assume the American people would prefer to have the most capable military mind in the Oval Office. In fact, if one relied solely on historical voting patterns, there was every reason to believe that, in this time of war, the only veteran on the 2008 campaign trail, John McCain, a genuine war hero, would have won the general election handily.

Several other factors, as we all know, were also in play to affect the outcome of the election. First of all, by the time the 2008 general election rolled around, war was not the first issue on the voters' minds. It was the economy, and John McCain had weakened his status on that issue, declaring publicly and early in the campaign that economics had never been one of his strong points. That remark came back to haunt the war hero.

Additionally, the country's engagement in two wars, a party image tarnished by a slew of highly publicized sex and ethics scandals, and the party's seeming abandonment of fiscal responsibility in favor of record spending left Republican voters less than inspired. McCain-Palin, though they consistently reinforced the theme that they were the natural candidates of reform, could not convince voters that their policies were different from the Bush administration's, by virtue of party affiliation alone.

To further add to McCain's GOP pains, he was never the candidate of the party's base. The party embraced him as the nominee because he was viewed as having the best chance given the national mood toward Republicans. This was not enough, however, to win over the suspicious conservative base. Senator McCain's positions on campaign finance reform and comprehensive immigration policies, which some right-wing pundits and activists labeled as amnesty, did not help him energize the rank-and-file GOP voters.

The economic instability further ignited voter sentiment to move beyond the status quo in pursuit of a new direction. While this naturally hurt the GOP, it also adversely affected Clinton.

No matter how often Clinton repeated the feminist mantra at campaign stops to underpin the historic nature of her campaign, her run, like McCain's, was rooted in the traditional patriarchal model of "toughness." Also like the McCain campaign, it was rooted in old technologies: there was nothing fresh and interesting and new about it, aside from the fact that Clinton happened to be a woman.

Interestingly, it seems that Clinton's campaign may have considered the option of letting her run "as a woman"—at the very least acknowledging the challenges she faced in being a woman in such a competition and what her victory could mean to healing old wounds—as Obama actually did when he addressed the same things in his now famous "race" speech.

Clinton's campaign *almost* took this step, at Clinton's urging. As Joshua Green reported in his in-depth analysis of the dysfunctional Clinton campaign for the *Atlantic*: "In the aftermath of Obama's historic race speech on March eighteenth, Sheila Jackson Lee, a Texas congresswoman, urged Clinton to deliver a speech of her own on gender.

"Clinton appeared very much to want to do this and solicited the advice of her staff, which characteristically split. The campaign went back and forth for weeks. Opponents argued that her oratory couldn't possibly match Obama's, and proponents countered that she would get credit simply for trying, would inspire legions of women to her cause, and would highlight an issue that everyone in the campaign fiercely believed was hurting them—sexism. But Clinton never made a decision, and she seemed troubled by the concern of Ann Lewis, perhaps her most venerable feminist adviser, who opposed such a speech for fear that it would equate sexism with racism—another contrast with Obama that Clinton feared she would lose."[9]

Instead, Clinton seemed overly fixated on showing the nation that she had the chops—on foreign policy, in particular—that she was "experienced" and "ready to lead." Her campaign, in fact, predicted that this would be the most important quality in the race. In November 2007, Clinton's senior strategist, Mark Penn, released a memo to "Interested Parties," which claimed "What is the most important card in this race? The leadership card. The voters are looking for someone who has the strength and experience to lead. . . . As Senator Clinton has said, change is just a word unless you have the strength and experience to make it happen."[10]

It's hard not to come to the conclusion that by running such a traditional campaign, layered and weighted down with traditional, patriarchal concerns, she wanted the voters to know that she was "safe."

Experience was never an issue. Voters could see her record of experience for themselves. They had the reference of her nearly two decades on the world stage; they didn't need that type of convincing. Polling data showed she always led on the "experience" questions. As has been discussed previously, MSNBC reported that with the Democratic field narrowed to two in early February, Clinton led on the question "Who would make the best commander in chief of the U.S. armed forces?" by fifteen points (50 percent to 35 percent).[11] And a Gallup poll out in March 2008 found that 65 percent of those polled thought Clinton "has the experience necessary to be president," while Obama polled at only 46 percent on the same question.[12]

Mark Penn and Ann Lewis did Clinton no favors by advising her to stick to what had been tried and true in politics for over 200 years—especially when she was, indeed, trying something that had so rarely ever before been tried in the modern age. Instead of openly embracing the freshness of Clinton's candidacy, they tried to camouflage that freshness with a coating of dust from the boys' stale old war room. This tactic proved even more fatal in the face of her opponent's ready embrace of his own differences, including racial, generational, and technological.

But Clinton's insistence on the "experience" message—on reminding us that she could "play with the boys"—not only reinforced gender stereotypes in an unhelpful way (Hey, a woman can be commander in chief too!), it turned people off—particularly younger voters, a key constituency that she needed and that was not responding to her static message. Her opponent had limited experience on the national stage and everyone knew it—*and Democratic primary voters didn't really care.* Unfortunately for Clinton, she and her team failed to respond effectively to what the data were consistently bearing out.

For example, the same Gallup poll that found that Clinton was leading Obama on the "experience" question by nearly twenty points also found that "experience" *wasn't all that important* a factor to many voters. Among Democrats surveyed, only 25 percent rated "experience" as the "most important characteristic" influencing their vote—behind "leadership and vision" (at 45 percent) and "issue positions" (at 29 percent). This pattern held for independents as well. As Gallup pointed out, "Americans are more likely to be looking for a candidate with leadership skills and vision, characteristics on which Obama has obvious strengths."[13]

And, in nearly every Democratic primary, voters rated "the ability to bring change" as more important than "experience." It was in states where those categories polled the tightest that Clinton was able to win. For example, as an ABC News analysis has shown (based on exit polls), Clinton won Ohio and Texas, where "the ability to bring needed change" beat "experience" as "the most important quality . . . by a seventeen point margin in Ohio and by fifteen points in Texas . . . [and both of these were] among the *fewest to pick change as the top attribute* in any primary this year." By contrast, in Vermont, where Obama won, the "change theme prevailed over experience by more than a thirty point margin, at the high end in primaries [to that point]."[14]

Even so, we can see that though Clinton was winning over voters who considered experience to be most important, those voters were outnumbered by voters who considered change to be the prevailing theme. The question that may never be satisfactorily answered is why, when Clinton's people had access to this very same polling data, they did not see the same phenomenon at work and adapt their campaign strategy to reflect what the voters were clearly telling them.

Even when Clinton did show glimmers of emotion—as in the obsessively reported "tears" incident in a Portsmouth, New Hampshire, coffee shop—rather than let that lead her into a discussion of anything new, she stuck to her olds guns. She circled right back to her ability to lead:

> Some people think elections are a game: who's up or who's down. . . . [welling up]. It's about our country. It's about our kids' future. It's about all of us together. Some of us put ourselves out there and do this against some difficult odds. . . . Some of us are right, and some of us are not. Some of us are ready, and some of us are not. . . . Some of us know what we will do on Day One, and some of us haven't thought that through.[15]

Interestingly—and, to her supporters, sadly—Clinton most effectively made the case for her embodiment of change in her final speech as a candidate—her concession speech in Washington on June 7, 2008:

> When I was asked what it means to be a woman running for president, I always gave the same answer: I was proud to be running as a women, but I was running because I thought I'd be the best president. . . . But I am a woman, and like millions of women, I know that there are still barriers and biases out there, often unconscious. And I want to build an America that respects and embraces the potential of every last one of us. We must make sure that women and men alike understand the struggles of their grandmothers and their mothers and that women enjoy equal pay and equal respect. Let us resolve and work toward achieving some very simple propositions: There are no acceptable limits and there are no acceptable prejudices in the twenty-first century in our country.[16]

Clearly, Clinton's inability or, perhaps, reluctance, to capture the change she represented—and that the country craved—was that much more striking in contrast to Obama's "transformational" message.

As in other cases, her campaign's weaknesses were exacerbated by the fact that they were so often Obama's strengths. This was, after all, the centerpiece of his campaign: hope and change and how he himself had lived it. He used his personal story to communicate not just who he was, but how it informed his view of the nation—and what needed to be done to make America better.

A campaign is never entirely about the issues at hand—those concerns the country faces as a whole community—but about which candidate can better communicate to this community his (or her!) vision of how it can face those issues and deal with them. Obama was not only better at the art of communication than Clinton was, but what he chose as the subject of his communication demonstrated an altogether more sophisticated grasp of what the voters were waiting to hear.

This is directly related to a key lesson to draw from Palin's candidacy: because the two instances when she spoke most directly to the broadest national audience (her convention speech and the vice presidential debate) were the ones in which she performed best. She was definitely different—brand new on the national scene, to most people, and to most a bold departure from Republican vice presidential candidates of the past. She was the Republicans' counterpunch to the change Obama represented and when she was candid and prepared, she could communicate that difference to her constituency brilliantly.

Why was she so effective on these two occasions, but not at all in other instances? Because she was able to combine the qualities that people "liked" about her—her connection to average American families, her ability to tell her own personal story in a compelling way, her friendly, optimistic, folksy demeanor—with a clear articulation of her (and, John McCain's) policy positions and governing philosophies.

Here's one example from her convention speech, laying out in clear and unpretentious language her complete governing philosophy:

> Politics isn't just a game of clashing parties and competing interests. The right reason is to challenge the status quo, to serve the common good, and to leave this nation better than we found it. No one expects us to agree on everything. But we are expected to govern with integrity, good will, clear convictions, and . . . a servant's heart. I pledge to all Americans that I will carry myself in this spirit as vice president of the United States. This was the spirit that brought me to the governor's office, when I took on the old politics as usual in Juneau . . . when I stood up to the special interests, the lobbyists, big oil companies, and the good-ol' boys network.[17]

And there is also this slightly different but quite effective example of Palin speaking from the heart about her infant son:

> From the inside, no family ever seems typical. That's how it is with us. Our family has the same ups and downs as any other . . . the same challenges and the same joys. Sometimes even the greatest joys bring challenge. And children with special needs inspire a special love. To the families of special-needs children all across this country, I have a message: For years, you sought to make

America a more welcoming place for your sons and daughters. I pledge to you that if we are elected, you will have a friend and advocate in the White House.[18]

Like Obama, she told us not only who she was, but how who she was helped to shape what she believed. Her personal story wasn't all she was—a trap she fell into later in the campaign. But her personal story was the foundation from which she would be able to promote policies she believed in and *lead*.

As I've already pointed out, it worked. To a point. Polls had the McCain-Palin ticket leading or tied with Obama-Biden immediately after the Republican National Convention, and much of the bump was due to women—especially white women who were able to directly identify with Palin's story and see themselves reflected in the candidate. The lead remained until the economic crash in mid-September, and the McCain team never recovered that lost ground.

The greater question is, why didn't we see *more* of this from Palin? Instead, we got too much rehashing of her personal story— the incessant claims to being "just a hockey mom" and a "maverick" for example—*without* the logical connections to how that would inform what she would do as vice president.

To be fair, given what McCain and Palin represented—the party of the incredibly unpopular incumbent president—*and* given the nation's economic turmoil, no amount of distancing short of a public rebuke of President Bush's policies, which would have been unadvised and devastatingly costly to their base, was likely to convince people that they represented a break from the past. But what each of the women candidates in this election possessed—their greatest assets—was buried by their respective campaigns in favor of what, clearly, their campaign managers saw as the more conventional attributes of presidential candidates.

As has been pointed out by many, Hillary Clinton's campaign was not just dysfunctional; it was a mess, nearly paralyzed by infighting and competing personalities and strategies.

The campaign seemed to jump from message to message without ever really settling on one—as the story about Congresswoman Sheila Jackson Lee illustrates. Indeed, by his own admission in his piece for the *Atlantic,* one of the reasons Joshua Green was able to get his hands on so many internal Clinton campaign documents is that competing staff factions fed them to him.

According to Green's five-page blockbuster, "The Front-Runner's Fall," Mark Penn, the presidential campaign's chief strategist, wrote in a memo to Clinton: "I cannot imagine America electing a president during a time of war who is not at his center fundamentally American in his thinking and in his values." Penn also suggested targeting Obama by focusing on the relationship with his controversial and outspoken pastor in a March 30 memo after Clinton's Texas and Ohio primary victories: "'Does anyone believe that it is possible to win the nomination without, over these next two months, raising all these issues on him? . . . Won't a single tape of [the Reverend Jeremiah] Wright going off on America with Obama sitting there be a game ender?'"[19]

An account of these damaging leaks was further reported by Mike Allen on August 10, 2008:

> *The Atlantic* Senior Editor Joshua Green writes that major decisions during her campaign for the Democratic presidential nomination would be put off for weeks until suddenly Clinton "would erupt, driving her staff to panic and misfire." Green reports that on a staff conference call in January where Clinton received "little response" or "silence" to several of her suggestions for how to recover from the Iowa loss and do better in New Hampshire, "Clinton began to grow angry, according to a participant's notes," Green recounts. "'This has been a very instructive call, talking to myself,' she snapped, and hung up."[20]

Damaging as this was, the campaign was dysfunctional in other ways as well. Penn, for example—and, remember, he was supposed to be the guy in charge—made some inexplicable and costly mistakes. *Time* magazine and others have reported one striking example: In an early strategy session Mark Penn confidently predicted that an early win in California would put her over the top because she would pick up all the state's 370 delegates. . . . [But of course,] Penn was wrong: Democrats, unlike the Republicans, apportion their delegates according to vote totals, rather than allowing any state to award them winner-take-all. Sitting nearby, veteran Democratic insider Harold M. Ickes, who had helped write those rules, was horrified—and let Penn know it. "How can it possibly be," Ickes asked, "that the much vaunted chief strategist doesn't understand proportional allocation?"[21]

If this story is accurate, and I have to assume it is, Clinton's entire campaign may have been based on a totally flawed approach. Needless to say, this is no way to run a railroad—with the train conductor unaware of the basic operating rules. Why didn't Clinton cut Penn loose then and there? Instead, he stayed until he was demoted, but only after his questionable lobbying ties came to light, in the final month of the primary season. By then, it was much too late to get the train back on the track again.

It's fair to ask who was really in control of the Clinton campaign—or maybe more to the point, why Clinton didn't manage it more directly and effectively. As has been widely reported, her campaign was effectively out of money in January 2008. Yes, *January*. Her strategy was almost completely dependent on her knocking out her rivals by February 5—which was mighty curious in light of her lackluster performance in and commitment to Iowa. Her mismanagement—and Obama's much vaunted "No drama Obama" management style—undercut whatever slim effect her message of experience might have had on voters who actually cared about that. Again, this is an example of a place where the weaknesses of Clinton's campaign was exacerbated by Obama's strengths.

When it came to Sarah Palin's campaign management, we are left to wonder if she was allowed—or insisted on—*any* control over her own media strategy in particular. Clearly, she was new to the national media scene. As a novice, a fact she was more than likely well aware of, she felt compelled to take the campaign staff's advice. But, come on. She was getting *killed* out there—and her own words were contributing to the bleeding. From "As for all that VP talk all the time, I tell ya I still can't answer that question until someone answers for me what exactly it is a VP does everyday" to this disheartening exchange with Katie Couric:

> *Couric:* You've said, quote, "John McCain will reform the way Wall Street does business." Other than supporting stricter regulations of Fannie Mae and Freddie Mac two years ago, can you give us any more example of his leading the charge for more oversight?
>
> *Palin:* I think that the example that you just cited, with his warnings two years ago about Fannie and Freddie—that, that's paramount. That's more than a heck of a lot of other senators and representatives did for us.
>
> *Couric:* But he's been in Congress for 26 years. He's been chairman of the powerful Commerce Committee. And he has almost always sided with less regulation, not more.
>
> *Palin:* He's also known as the maverick though, taking shots from his own party, and certainly taking shots from the other party. Trying to get people to understand what he's been talking about—the need to reform government.
>
> *Couric:* But can you give me any other concrete examples? Because I know you've said Barack Obama is a lot of talk and no action. Can you give me any other examples in his 26 years of John McCain truly taking a stand on this?
>
> *Palin:* I can give you examples of things that John McCain has done, that has shown his foresight, his pragmatism, and his leadership abilities. And that is what America needs today.
>
> *Couric:* I'm just going to ask you one more time—not to belabor the point. Specific examples in his 26 years of pushing for more regulation.
>
> *Palin:* I'll try to find you some and I'll bring them to you.[22]

Did no one on the McCain campaign have the experience to anticipate some of the standard questions his vice presidential candidate might have to field and the foresight to assist her in preparing answers for them? It might have been error enough for the McCain staff to misread Palin's strengths and to use her in ways that didn't allow her natural abilities to shine, but it compounded the error exponentially not to prepare her adequately for the limited venues where they did allow her to appear.

The bottom line? Obama may not have been the most experienced candidate, but he out-campaigned them all—using new technologies to his advantage (especially in terms of fundraising), honing in on the message Americans were most hungry to hear and delivering it to them with exceptional oratorical skills, and keeping tight control of how that message was delivered by a disciplined campaign staff.

But these weren't the only reasons Barack Obama was able to succeed. That his victories in 2008—both in the primaries and the general election—were due in large measure to young people connecting with his message has been well documented. What is less clear is why his opponents—particularly Hillary Clinton—did not realize this soon enough.

Even before 2008, the writing was on the wall. According to the nonpartisan Center for Information and Research on Civic Learning and Engagement (CIRCLE), in 2004 "voter turnout among young people reached its highest level in more than a decade" following "a steady decline since 1972, with the exception of a spike in turnout in 1992."[23]

Moreover, this increase in voting turnout among young people was especially striking among *young women*, especially those who were single. "The 2004 election saw greater increases in voting among single young people than among married ones, as *turnout for single females age 18–24 increased 12 percentage points, or about a third, since 2000*" (emphasis added). This increase was apparent *across racial lines*: in "2000 and 2004, there is no significant difference in the turnout rate of young African-American women and young white women," and though the voting rate of young Latina women was lower overall, it was still ticking upward.

This was also true among young women at every level of educational attainment. Although women with a bachelor's degree or higher were still the most likely group to vote overall, turnout among young women of all levels of educational achievement was trending sharply upward.[24]

Repeat after me: young women!

And, of course, young women have historically voted Demo-cratic. They voted for the 2004 Democratic nominee John F. Kerry in large numbers—women aged 18–29 voted for Kerry 56 percent to President Bush's 43 percent. And, according to surveys in 2002 and 2004, "young women are more likely than their young male counterparts to feel they could make a difference in their commu-nities. Research has shown that young people who feel that they can make a difference, or feel efficacious, are more likely to vote."[25]

Even more to my point is this: "young women are more likely to identify themselves as moderates than their young male counterparts." This is something that should have played directly to Clinton's strengths, had she recognized the trend in time.[26]

Why she didn't is anyone's guess. The importance of young voters—especially women—was certainly clear before, say, the Iowa caucuses in 2008. Indeed, her own husband's campaign in 1992 should have made plain to Clinton the potential importance of young voters.

But Iowa brought the issue into sharp focus. Overall, Demo-cratic turnout in Iowa was up by 90 percent, but "the number of young Democrats participating soared one hundred and thirty-five per cent." It should have tipped off somebody in Clinton's cam-paign when this statistic was revealed: these "young voters pre-ferred Obama over the next-closest competitor by more than four to one. [They] gave the Illinois Senator a net gain of some 17,000 votes; Obama finished roughly 20,000 votes ahead of former Sen-ator John Edwards and Senator Hillary Clinton."[27] In the starkest sense, the youth vote was responsible for Obama's victory—and the end of Clinton's inevitability.

So, how did he do it? How did Obama attract all these young people, particularly young women, to him?

Obama's message of change and hope surely contributed. But, as others have pointed out, "Obama applied lessons learned—re-learned—in recent years about the importance of face-to-face grassroots organizing."[28] As one Obama supporter, Mike Draper, twenty-four, from Des Moines told MTV, "Obama's win shows that when you have an authentic, great candidate who promises to bring change and to bring out people, and they actually do it, they can win. In every precinct I went to, they said that double the people came out than they expected."[29]

This anecdotal evidence fits almost precisely with the academic research conducted since 2004. In 2006, the George Washington University Graduate School of Political Management issued a report called "Young Voter Mobilization Tactics," which was a compilation of recent research on turning out the youth vote. Pulling from a slew of studies, the report found several key themes for attracting eighteen- to twenty-nine-year-old voters, including:

- Quality counts: Actual votes per contact will be higher when the contact is more personalized and interactive. [In particular, the report found that "canvassing has the greatest impact on turning out young people to vote."]
- Begin with the basics: Young people need nuts-and-bolts practical information about how to vote. And efforts that make voting more convenient are quite effective.
- The medium matters more than the message. [The report concluded that, "to date, the growing body of experimental research has not found that any type of message works better than another. It is more about making a quality contact."]
- Young people are easy to incorporate into your lists and turnout programs. Excluding young voters from your turnout efforts is a mistake.
- Ethnic and immigrant youth are cost-effective targets.
- Initial mobilization makes for repeat voters—Parties, candidates and interest groups should expect long-term benefits from mobilizing youth today.[30]

I quote this study in detail in part because it essentially offers a retrospective playbook for how the Obama camp won the youth vote in Iowa and across the nation. And this report and all the data and studies it was based on were available well in advance of the 2008 campaign season. Both the McCain campaign and the Clinton campaign could have had access to the same information that Obama used so successfully.

Of course, Obama's triumph with young voters continued after Iowa and throughout the primary season. "Obama won the 18-to-29 demographic by 4–1 in Iowa, 3–1 in New Hampshire, 3–1 in South Carolina and 2–1 in Nevada, and he trounced Clinton, often by as much as 50 percent among young voters, in ten of the thirteen Super Tuesday states with available data."[31] Overall, for the states in which there was exit polling data available, over 5 million young people (age 18–29) voted in the Democratic primaries, and an overwhelming 60 percent went for Obama (with 38 percent for Clinton).[32]

In the general election, an estimated 23 million young Americans under the age of thirty voted, an increase of 3.4 million compared with 2004.[33] Obama would win 61 percent of these young voters, according to Gallup (though some estimates have ranged even higher) and 53 percent of 30–49-year-olds. The only age group that McCain won was 65+ (54 percent to Obama's 46 percent).[34]

The lesson for future candidates, particularly Democrats, from Obama's overwhelming success with young voters is twofold. First, his message was tuned in not only to the national mood, but to the "youth mood." He understood what should be obvious—that young people are idealistic—and he knew that they were more likely to view voting as a way to bring about change.

This is something that has been increasingly true in recent elections. Young people viewed Obama as someone who was authentic and understood them and the issues important to them. Beyond the need to address certain economic issues during the campaign, was it really a coincidence that "the economy" was identified by young voters as their top issue as well as one of Obama's consistent talking points on every stump stop? Indeed, as CIRCLE reported, "young people were much more likely than others to feel that Obama was in touch with people like themselves: 69 percent of young voters versus 57 percent of all voters."[35]

And second, in addition to his ability to zero in on the exact issues that were on young people's minds, Obama's campaign tactics—from his interactive Internet presence and fundraising machine to his focus on face-to-face outreach and young volunteers, an outreach that was not limited just to college campuses—gave him the edge. Not only did young people vote in large numbers for Obama, they were less likely to have been contacted by the McCain campaign.

CIRCLE reported that "Young people were slightly more likely than older people to be contacted by someone on behalf of the Obama campaign (16 percent versus 13 percent of the entire electorate). But they were less likely than others to be contacted on behalf of the McCain campaign: 4 percent versus 6 percent of the entire electorate."[36]

I think it goes without saying that for Republican candidates the lessons are even more ominous. Republicans are losing the youth vote—women and men—even as those voters are becoming more energized and more likely to vote. In fact, the breakdown of the groups that the Republicans lost in the 2008 election should be taken as a stern warning for the next GOP candidate. The McCain-Palin ticket lost among women, among all age groups except those sixty-five and older, in all regions except the South (where they were tied). They won white voters (by about an eight-point spread), split the overall male vote 50-50, and essentially split the religious vote (although Biden probably provided a nice bump among Catholics). McCain-Palin lost independent voters (though it was close), but among self-described "moderates" they were hammered 63 percent to 37 percent.[37]

This does not add up to good news for the Republicans. Put simply, the whiter, older, and more male the Republican Party becomes—both in terms of candidates and supporters—the less successful the party will be. Message does matter, but so does *how* we deliver it and *who* does the delivering. It's not just the message—it's the messenger and the method.

Which brings me to another vital point: the crucial importance of social networking through digital technologies in the future of successful campaigning, particularly as it relates to young people. I'm talking beyond the blogosphere, though that is a critical realm, to include Facebook, Google Groups, YouTube, Twitter, Fark, and whatever comes next.

If it wasn't already clear before the 2008 election, it must be now. The effect for a political candidate who is unprepared to successfully utilize such social media on a national and local level is immediate and disastrous. It's like a Swiftboat ad on steroids.

Neither the Clinton nor the McCain-Palin team was out in front on this, and the lack was particularly damaging for Palin because she was so new. She was unknown—and thus undefined—to the majority of American voters of both parties. So, defining who she was—swiftly and eagerly—became job number one for her team and her opponents. The push had to be immediate—as did any responses to unfair criticism that Palin received.

Anticipating the crush, at least one person was thinking ahead of the social media curve. As reported by the *New York Times,* someone greatly expanded and revised Palin's entry on Wikipedia in the days just prior to her selection. Though the writer did a good job and was initially complimented by other Wikipedia editors, it became a mini-controversy once the writer acknowledged they volunteered for the McCain campaign.[38]

But in general, there was too long a lag, and liberals in particular were far more effective at using blogs and other social media to define Palin for the rest of the country.

As Camille Paglia wrote on Salon.com:

Over the Labor Day weekend, with most of the big enchiladas of the major media on vacation, the vacuum was filled with a hallucinatory hurricane in the leftist blogosphere, which unleashed a grotesquely lurid series of allegations, fantasies, half-truths and outright lies about Palin. What a tacky low in American politics—which has already caused a backlash that could damage Obama's campaign. . . . To automatically assume that she is a religious fanatic who has embraced the most extreme ideas of her local church is exactly the kind of careless reasoning that has been unjustly applied to Barack Obama.[39]

This predicted backlash against Obama's campaign didn't materialize—or, if it did initially, it didn't stick. And the reason it didn't have staying power was at least in part because of the ineffective electronic response from the McCain-Palin team.

As Leslie Bradshaw, director of engagement at New Media Strategies (NMS), a market leader in social media marketing and measurement, told me, "the density and frequency of the hyper-news-cycle and hyper-social nature of today's media speeds up the process to authenticate" a candidate.[40] Palin was quickly and severely authenticated as *incompetent*. That was the narrative that took off.

Not only did the McCain campaign not counter this argument forcefully by using social media effectively, its own media strategy seemed to play into it. By keeping Palin under wraps for so long, they let everyone else tell us who she was—and, as I've already detailed, they essentially created a situation where Palin was probably unable to ever effectively break out of that mold—even with the most flawless debate performance, for example, which she did not give.

As a telling example of just how effective—or, depending on your view, how disastrous—social media can be for defining a candidate, especially one who is relatively new to the scene, I turned to NMS. They conducted an independent analysis of the 2008 election cycle, including the moment that *Saturday Night Live*'s Tina Fey and Amy Poehler began their parody of the Sarah Palin–Katie Couric interview. They concluded that Internet users' fascination with Sarah Palin began as soon as she was named John McCain's running mate. On the day of Palin's announcement, her Wikipedia article was visited 2.5 million times. Palin's name was searched more often in 2008 than that of any other politician, except Barack Obama, and far more than McCain himself. What's more, Google users sought more information about Palin than about any other woman.

One of the more noteworthy developments was that Tina Fey's impression of Palin boosted Fey's popularity significantly. The number of blog posts written about Sarah Palin nearly doubled from August to September, while the number of posts about Tina Fey more than tripled. The trend continued after the election. For instance, on Twitter through July 2009, Palin was mentioned in more than 1.8 million separate Twitter posts (tweets), while Fey's name appeared in more than thirty thousand. Interestingly, the last names of both appeared in more than ten thousand tweets, indicating that Fey's association with Palin via her *SNL* character continues to be very strong.[41]

The lessons for future candidates for any office are clear. But that doesn't mean that traditional media tactics aren't still vitally important, or that they can be overlooked. Conservative talk radio is one example. In some ways, the explosion of social media—especially blogs—from progressives and liberals can be viewed as a reaction to the rise of conservative talk radio in the 1990s. Democrats were often frustrated in election cycles by the power of radio talk show hosts to turn out voters—and to turn people on to their ideas.

Take Rush Limbaugh: today, his listenership is estimated to range between 12.5 and 20 million.[42] But also keep in mind that Limbaugh's listeners are mostly men—62 percent of them, according to a Pew study. And they are older than the national average—with 52 percent of Limbaugh's listeners in the 50+ age category. Similarly, 58 percent of viewers of Bill O'Reilly's *The O'Reilly Factor* on FOX News, are over 50 years of age. Compare that with, say, *The Daily Show*, where only 23 percent of viewers are over the age of 50, although 66 percent are male.[43]

As the Nielsen Company recently reported, blogs and other social media (so-called member communities) are growing like wildfire—here and around the world. "Now visited by over two-thirds (67 percent) of the global online population, 'member communities,' which include both social networks and blogs, has become the fourth most popular online category—ahead of personal email. It is growing twice as fast as any of the other four largest sectors (search, portals, PC software and email)."

The study also confirmed that the reach of social media is extending beyond just the youngest demographics, "becoming more diverse in terms of age: the biggest increase in visitors during 2008 to 'member community' web sites globally came from the 35–49 year old age group, with an increase of over 11.3 million!"[44]

Whether candidates like it or not, they absolutely must build up their online and social capital in advance of their candidacies, with a particular focus on influencing people who are already active on the Internet. And they must have an army of supporters prepared to use social media effectively and relentlessly as soon as the campaign begins. This would be a lesson Palin would later learn the hard way, when she attempted to use Twitter to build a buzz for her resignation press conference. Unfortunately, she appeared "goofy" and unfocused and her opponents used the erratic posts to further label Palin as "a quitter" who is "unsuitable for higher office."

The truth is, even if a candidate resists these new technologies and methods of communication, her opponents won't, and, clearly, using these new tools without a full grasp of their power and impact can do more harm than good.

5

FROM THE KITCHEN TO THE KITCHEN CABINET

*I*F YOU TALK POLITICS in your family, as I do in mine, you have probably been part of at least one conversation over the last twenty-five years about whether the United States is "ready" for a woman president and when that is likely to happen. The 2008 election certainly brought a new urgency and focus to many of these discussions, which really involve two distinct questions: The first—is America ready to elect a woman president?—is more theoretical. The second—would you personally vote for a woman to be president (or vice president)?—brings the focus home.

While the discussion over your family dinner table might be more or less contentious, when you look at the data, it seems that overall the answer to both questions is yes.

Theoretically, Americans appear prepared to elect a woman president. A March 2008 CBS News poll found that 59 percent of those surveyed believe America is ready for a woman president. That's not exactly overwhelming, but it is generally consistent, if a bit on the low side, with what other national polls have recorded. A June 2008 CNN poll showed 67 percent responded affirmatively to the question, "Do you think America is ready for a woman president or not?" And the NBC–*Wall Street Journal* poll, also from March 2008, found 71 percent of respondents agreeing that "voters of this country are ready to elect a qualified woman as president."

The number of people saying the country is *ready* for a woman president is significantly less than the number of people, 92 percent, who say they would *vote* for a woman president. But both groups appear to constitute a majority of the electorate.

Asking someone if they would *vote* for a woman for the nation's highest office is an altogether more personal question—and answers to that question vary year to year and poll to poll. Recall the ABC News–*Washington Post* poll from chapter 1 that found that 84 percent of people said that they themselves would be "entirely" (62 percent) or "somewhat" (22 percent) comfortable with "a woman president of the United States."[1] So, as it is with other polling trends, Americans ascribe to themselves more of a willingness to support a woman president than they do to their fellow citizens. In other words: it's not about me, it's about them.

Even as they are more likely to support the idea of a woman president, however, more Americans view gender as a bigger barrier to presidential leadership than race. At the same time, they see racism as a bigger problem for the nation than sexism. It's an odd paradox, but the numbers bear it out. A CBS News poll conducted in the midst of the 2008 primaries found that "42 percent of respondents said racism is a 'serious problem' in the country compared to just 10 percent who said the same of sexism." The same poll found that "39 percent of registered voters said a woman running for president faces more obstacles while 33 percent said a black candidate does."[2]

Those statistics make for a bit of a conundrum, don't they? Logically, it would seem, that if racism actually were the bigger problem, then black politicians would have the harder time getting into office. Flipping it around then, if sexism is such a small problem—if only 10 percent think it's a problem at all—then women should face very few obstacles on their runs for elected office. You have to wonder if this is another manifestation of the "It's not about me, it's about them" way people tend to respond to polls. I certainly wonder about the breakdown of the respondents to those questions. Were the people who thought racism was a great obstacle from a disproportionately black sampling? Were the people who thought sexism was almost a nonissue disproportionately men? But one thing we do know from the results of other polls is that it is women, in particular, who feel that female politicians get an unfair shake.

According to a poll of women conducted for Lifetime Networks after the 2008 election, "65 percent of women—majorities in *every* demographic and political group—said that male and female candidates are held to different standards on the campaign trail." Women thought it was easier for a man to be "taken seriously by the voters," to be "covered seriously by the media," and to "address issues such as national security and terrorism," as well as "address the issue of the economy."[3] Again, these are results that set me to wondering: if a woman candidate had not been brought to national attention as a "babe," a "honey," or "my heartthrob," would that have made the public view her with more gravitas than they did in the midst of all the gushing about her physical attributes?

But in general, what we can take away from these last few statements is that women, while not necessarily believing a woman shouldn't be president, believed that people ascribed credibility to a man that a woman would not automatically enjoy. But does this influence their voting behavior—are women more likely to support female candidates for political office?

Before we take a look at some of the additional research on this subject, let's take a look at some empirical results from the recent congressional elections. According to an analysis prepared by Nate Silver on the Fivethirtyeight blog, about 17 percent of the nation's 538 congressional districts (including the territories and Washington, D.C.) elected a woman the last time they were given the opportunity to do so.[4]

Silver used population data to rank the congressional districts and states by the gender of the voting population. What he discovered is that nine of the 25 most male-dominated districts (which represent 36 percent of the total) most recently elected a woman to office, as compared with four of the 25 most female-dominated districts.

"This alone is somewhat interesting," Silver writes, "however, it actually conceals the strength of the relationship because female-dominated districts are more likely to vote Democratic, and Democratic-leaning districts are more likely to elect women to office regardless of their sex ratios."

"It's possible, and maybe even somewhat likely, that there is some sort of latent variable affecting both the sex ratios and elections to the Congress that I haven't accounted for," Silver's analysis concludes. "If this really is being driven by the sex ratios, however, and it's being driven in this extremely counterintuitive way, it's one of the more fascinating things that I've come across.

"Perhaps in male-dominated areas, women are more likely to violate traditional sex roles including something like running for political office, which has traditionally been a male-dominated occupation—the Sarah Palin frontierswoman caricature works well here. It would be interesting to know whether there are more women actually running for office in male-dominated areas, or rather, whether they are winning more often when they do run. Or perhaps this is a phenomenon that goes beyond politics, and career growth is retarded for the dominant gender when there is an insufficient number of the opposite one. Or perhaps there is even something more Freudian: a lack of female companionship (or vice versa) triggers a yearning for it that is manifested in the way we vote," he writes.

The Pew Research Center for the People & the Press put this question to the test in 2007 and found that the gender gap tends to help women running for office as Democrats—but not women running as Republicans, which would seem to support Silver's findings.

Pew analyzed the voting patterns for candidates for U.S. senator and for governor in recent years. They looked at, for example, "exit polls from forty senatorial and gubernatorial elections since 1998 in which a female Democratic candidate faced a male Republican . . . [and found that on] average, the female Democratic candidates captured the votes of 55 percent of women compared with 47 percent of men." This gap was similar, they pointed out, to the gender gap that Hillary Clinton enjoyed at the time in a fictitious head-to-head match-up with Republican Rudy Giuliani.

But Pew also concluded that there "are no signs that female Republican candidates receive a similar advantage. In the fifteen races observed where a female Republican faced a male Democrat . . . women voted for female Republican candidates about as often as they did for male Republicans."[5] These results force a basic question: Why don't female Republican candidates enjoy women's support? As a Republican, this is a question I believe needs to be taken seriously by party leaders.

The gender gap appears to hold true for 2008, at least as far as Republicans are concerned. The "Palin Pick" initially resulted in a surge of support from women—white women, in particular—but that uptick of support did not hold. "The effect of Sarah Palin is not one that has been long lasting in terms of shifting the dynamics of the gender gap," Susan J. Carroll of Rutgers University's Center for American Women and Politics told Politico.com. Her colleague, Debbie Walsh, said that the shift back toward Obama reflects that "the gender gap is not about the gender of the candidate, it's about the issues. . . . We certainly have seen that the gaps have been widening during the economic issue. . . . [W]omen are more economically vulnerable even in the best of times."[6]

While it eludes me how women, as a group, could have failed to get behind Palin—someone who so very clearly reflected the lifestyle choices, hard work ethic, and traditional values that so many women admire and seek to emulate—in the end, women went for Obama-Biden in large numbers, reinforcing the traditional gender-gap advantage for Democrats, while Obama and McCain essentially split the male vote. To review the numbers, overall 56 percent of women voted for Obama-Biden versus 43 percent for McCain-Palin. Obama's percentage of women was higher than Senator John Kerry's 51 percent in 2004. More white women (46 percent) voted for Obama than did white men (42 percent); more Latina women (68 percent) voted for Obama than did Latino men (64 percent); and both black women (96 percent) and black men (95 percent) overwhelmingly supported Obama. [7]

Among unmarried women (single, separated, divorced, or widowed), Obama won 70 percent to 29 percent; while married women voted for McCain by a much slimmer margin—50 percent to 47 percent.[8] And *young* women were more likely to vote than young men. In 2008, young women accounted for 55 percent of the votes among 18- to 29-year-olds, and for young African American voters, women made up 62 percent of the voters.[9]

We also have state-by-state data to compare from the 2008 election (based on entrance polling). As has been discussed, Clinton lost the women's vote in the Iowa caucuses (30 percent to Obama's 33 percent, according to Politico.com[10]), but she won women in New Hampshire—where they make up 57 percent of the voters—by 12 points.[11]

So it seems that we can say with some degree of certainty (at least based on recent elections) that women may be more likely to vote for Democrats—as white men are more likely to vote for Republicans—but it's not necessarily clear that women are more willing to vote for women because they are women. Why is that? The answers to these questions, as well as the questions themselves, restate the point of this book. What kept the majority of women from backing the ticket that had embraced the woman candidate? Was it the issues? Was it that McCain had made the unfortunate comment that portrayed him as less than knowledgeable about the economy at a time when the economy was thrust to the forefront of the voters' concerns? Was it that voters were simply unwilling to separate the candidates from the unpopular policies of the previous administration? Or was something more insidious going on?

If we are ready for a woman president—and let's concede, please, that we are—the next logical question to ask is what voters want and expect from women in positions of leadership.

This answer, again, appears to differ based on the party affiliation. A Pew study conducted in the summer of 2008—*before* the introduction of Sarah Palin—found that "Republicans are significantly less likely to vote for a candidate who is a mother of young children than one who is a father of young children, other factors being equal. Barely one-in-five, just 21 percent of Republicans said they were very likely to support a candidate for U.S. Congress who was the mother of school-aged children, while 31 percent said they would support a father who had the identical personal and career profile."

This did not hold for Democrats, and indeed had the opposite effect, especially among women: "Democratic women in particular more strongly supported Ann the mother [a hypothetical candidate for Congress] than Andrew the father (36 percent versus 19 percent). Among Democratic men, neither gender nor parenthood made a difference."[12]

This is just one more study, obviously, and it seems at least plausible that Palin's candidacy—and her decision to address some of the biases we hold about women with young children head on, as former New York City mayor Rudy Giuliani did when he introduced her to the Republican convention—may have changed these ideas, especially among Republicans. I believe it probably has. At least, I hope that's true, and the support of the party's base for Palin's candidacy seems to suggest that it is. But it does raise the question of whether or not the fact that Palin did have young children steered some voters away from her camp.

This is a point to ponder: Will it be possible for the first woman president or vice president of the United States to have young children? And it's a fair question. After all, it was only forty years ago that Hollywood's *Kisses for My President* concluded with the first woman chief executive of the United States resigning from office when she finds out she is pregnant.

Consider the way Sarah Palin was treated in comparison to House Speaker Nancy Pelosi (D-CA). Palin was routinely and, in my view, unfairly attacked over the possible effect her election to the vice presidency might have on her children. Contrast this with the way Pelosi's election as the first woman to be Speaker of the U.S. House of Representatives was greeted in January 2007.

Now it is true that Pelosi didn't have to win a national campaign to get the job. And it is also true that she is not subject to the same level of scrutiny; whether she should be is a different matter. In any event, the more obvious difference between Palin and Pelosi is that Pelosi's children are not only grown, but she also is a grandmother. Which requires us to consider whether a woman candidate with children the same age as, say, Obama's children could ever expect Americans to vote for her in numbers great enough to elect her to the presidency. Would the nation be willing to elect a mother with young children in the Oval Office as they have shown, not infrequently in the past, that they are willing to elect a father with young children?

This discussion raises another interesting paradox: if we assume, for the sake of plausible argument, that our first woman president will have already raised her children (or perhaps will have chosen not to have children, which is unlikely—as among the seminal life events modern voters seem to demand of a candidate from either party is to have married and had children), she would presumably be at least middle-aged.

That would fly in the face of another trend: the growing importance of younger voters (and correspondingly younger candidates). The 2008 election provided examples of two candidates—Barack Obama and Sarah Palin—both in their forties, both with young families, and both projecting an air of being beyond the struggles of their parents' generation—"postfeminist" or "postracial."

The accuracy of these labels is, of course, arguable. But, anecdotally, it seemed to appear that way to an awful lot of voters. It was these young voters in particular who went over-whelmingly for Obama-Biden, as has been discussed, because of their belief that Obama better understood their concerns. What was it about these candidates, and their life experiences, that convinced these young voters that Obama better reflected their life experiences?

Consider the life experience a viable woman candidate would be expected to have. First, of course, is executive and legislative experience.

Much that had been written and said about Obama's relative lack of experience on the national political stage would not have been glossed over had the candidate in question been a woman with similar credentials. As Dee Dee Myers, the first woman to serve as White House press secretary, told the *Guardian,* referring to Obama's "two years in the senate and eight years in the state legislature . . . I think people would have [told a woman], 'What are you, sweetie? Go home and get yourself some experience.'"[13]

Certainly Sarah Palin's experiences as a mayor and governor were not seen as sufficient preparation for the office she sought—and we heard a lot about it from her detractors. Though being a governor has certainly helped a few other presidential candidates (like Clinton, Carter, Bush 43, and Reagan) Palin's lack of a national reputation hurt her. I believe this was at least in part because there is a different level of notoriety—a national comfort level—that women must achieve before they can be considered safe. Call it a different acceptance curve for women, and let's lay it on the table very specifically as the curve relates to the 2008 presidential race: two years in national politics was good enough for Obama, but not for Palin.

The experience question is one reason some have given for why other countries around the world—particularly those with parliamentary systems—have seen women leaders rise to the top, while the United States has not. "A parliament permits women to rise gradually up the ranks to head a political party, while accu-mulating a record of achievement and building a base of support among fellow legislators."[14] Again, it all hinges on this notion of acceptance—she's been around a while and met the test; we're comfortable with her.

This idea of a different acceptance curve for women presidential candidates augers for the potential of a woman with an established national presence—and leadership reputation—to come from the corporate sector. If she has children, the idea that she has already successfully balanced work-life issues in the cutthroat corporate world would bode well with those voters who can't stomach putting a mom in the White House. And, the fact that she would also (likely) be wealthy wouldn't hurt her chances either—or her ability to fund (or raise money for) her campaign.

A 2005 study by Caliper, titled "The Qualities That Distinguish Women Leaders," found some interesting traits shared by very successful women executives. The year-long study, based in part on interviews with fifty-nine women leaders in nineteen business sectors in the United Kingdom and the United States, found that women leaders "are more persuasive than their male counterparts," "feel the sting of rejection, learn from adversity and carry on with an 'I'll show you' attitude," "have an inclusive, team building leadership style of problem solving and decision making," and "are more likely to ignore rules and take risks."[15]

But even though those may sound like promising attributes in a political candidate as well, it's unclear what exactly we expect from women candidates in terms of temperament—that all important "personality" factor. I'm tempted to say it doesn't matter. But that's obviously wishful thinking. It matters—way too much.

Hilary Lips of Radford University in Virginia writes, "It appears that the acceptable scripts for women in powerful public political roles are still rigidly defined and easy to violate—by being too 'pushy' or too 'soft,' too 'strident' or too accommodating, too sexless or too sexual. . . . With the necessity to conform to two, often conflicting, sets of expectations, high-profile women leaders in the United States are relentlessly held to a higher standard than their male counterparts."[16]

This is not some ancillary concern of modern campaigns, either. Hillary Clinton is perhaps the poster woman for this "personality test." As a senior Democratic operative and long-time Clinton adviser told me, when Hillary Clinton was *first* considering her own political future—in the 1990s—the concern about her likability was paramount, particularly among the *men* advising her. They were not overly concerned about whether Clinton would be taken seriously as a possible commander in chief. No, they were much more concerned that "Nobody likes you."

Clinton was even asked about this issue—as we saw in chapter 2—about whether or not she was likable enough during a debate in New Hampshire (though her male opponents were spared the Miss Congeniality question), and famously responded (to well-deserved laughs): "Well, that hurts my feelings . . . but I'll try to go on."[17]

It's true that there's this pressure on women candidates to "be nice"—or, at least, nicer than your average male politician. As CNN senior political correspondent Candy Crowley asked, "Why do women as candidates have to go on a warm and fuzzy tour?"[18] It's not just going on ABC's *The View* or *Oprah*. It's also this incessant need to trot out every elementary school teacher, coach, best friend, and family member for an interview. That may be a slight exaggeration—but you get my drift.

To put it another and more scholarly way, Lips has argued that "women are often required to 'soften' their leadership styles to gain the approval of their constituents. . . . Women who do not temper their agency and competence with warmth and friendliness risk being disliked and less influential; men face no such necessity to be agreeable while exercising power."[19]

As Hilary Rosen said to me, "I am very much of the school that women have to work harder, be more present, be more engaged, be more creative than men do to succeed in the same job. Period. I think it's true for African Americans, for Latinos, for women, for any minority. And, on top of being stellar in all of these areas, we have to be really, really nice, too."[20]

And this need for an "image tour" has become an absolute requirement for the wives of presidential candidates. Michelle Obama's turn on *The View* in June 2008 was widely seen as an attempt to soften her image, damaged by her "proud of my country" remarks. She jokingly greeted each *View* co-host with a "fist-bump, please," and said that she was "proud of my country, without a doubt, adding that nowhere but in America could my story be possible. . . . [And] what I was talking about is pride in the political process." She also praised then First Lady Laura Bush and Hillary Clinton, saying, "People aren't used to strong women. . . . We don't even know what to say about them. . . . It's only when women like [Clinton] take the hits and it's painful, it's hurtful, but she's taking them so that my girls, when they come along, won't have to feel it as badly."[21] Some saw this new woman-to-woman solidarity with Clinton as gracious, others as ironic because during the time when her husband was trying to beat Clinton in a primary race, Mrs. Obama certainly did not come to Clinton's defense.

Even more ironically, though she was ultimately unsuccessful, Hillary Clinton did appear to have met the acceptance test.

In addition to leading her opponents on the "experience" factor throughout the primaries, her years in the Senate were viewed favorably by many Americans. One instructive poll was conducted by Gallup in 2006 and examined a set of reasons why Americans would (or would not) vote for Hillary Clinton for president. The fact that "she has served as a senator representing New York since 2001" was the top reason cited to vote for Hillary Clinton, with 42 percent of people responding positively and 17 percent saying it would be a reason to vote against her. Forty-eight percent of women said this would be a reason to support her—the top response given by women.

The other leading reasons included "she was a prominent attorney before becoming First Lady" (34 percent overall, 40 percent of women), "she has called on the Democratic Party to take a more moderate stance on abortion" (33 percent overall, 33 percent of women), and "she would be the first woman president," (32 percent overall, 39 percent of women).

And many thought she was qualified for—or even deserved—the Democratic vice presidential spot. Even Joe Biden conceded as much after his own selection to the Democratic ticket, saying at a roundtable meeting in Nashua, New Hampshire, that "Hillary Clinton is as qualified or more qualified than I am to be vice president of the United States of America. Quite frankly, it might have been a better pick than me. . . . She's qualified to be president. I mean that sincerely, she's first rate."[22]

Part of the reason, in my view, that Clinton's own campaign undermined her chances is that either she or her staff seemed to distrust these sorts of poll results. Maybe they didn't believe that people really would accept a woman for president or really would accept that she was qualified enough. They also remained convinced that the election was about "experience" for far too long. Remember "change versus more of the same"? They apparently didn't. And, as a result, they beat us over the head with experience—continually selling us on her ability to be "ready on day one," even as polls (and voters themselves) were screaming for change and vision.

It's part of the overall paradox of Hillary Clinton's candidacy. The first woman with a real shot at the Oval Office was not seen as representing a change. She was the establishment candidate, the Democratic insider—"inevitable," as we were so often told by the major media, which in retrospect serves as the primary piece of irony we can all take away from the 2008 campaigns.

As Vicki Haddock of the *San Francisco Chronicle* wrote, "It's as if in the last half-century, the notion of a female president went from heretical to banal without ever having become, you know, reality."[23]

At least in 2008 it wasn't to be. We were done with Clintons and Bushes. Let's give the new kid a shot—or more precisely, the new guy.

Where are we, then? In light of this discussion we've just had, let me pose here some of the questions we'll take on and try to answer in the last chapter of this book, the primary one being: What will a winning woman candidate have to do, be, and look like in order to win a national election?

Unlike men, who, no matter their ethnic background, have very similar life expectancies of full-time work, women have vastly different life experiences. Most marry, but some don't. Most have children, but some don't. Of those who have children, some are stay-at-home moms; others work either full time or part time. Young mothers who stay at home with their children often look down on young mothers who work, their views shaped by the perspective that these working moms aren't putting their kids first. Working mothers, on the other hand, some of whom may *have* to work to help support their families, may feel jealous of the moms who have the luxury of spending their child's formative years as full-time moms. Who can unite these voters with such dissimilar life experiences into a reliable voting bloc? What does the winning woman candidate look like and—importantly—what does her family life look like?

As one senior Democratic advisor told me when we were discussing Clinton's candidacy, postelection:

> Women for Hillary have always been complicated. Back in the Senate race in 2000, we did a bunch of focus groups with women and it was fascinating. Some women were upset with her because she stayed with her husband. Some women were proud because she stayed. Some women were threatened by her. Some thought she was a bitch because she was very ambitious. It was very complicated. It wasn't based on her strength as a candidate or strength on the issues. It was all based on her personal psychological imprint. They wanted to get deep into her psyche.

However deep into Clinton's psyche these voters may have wanted to go, what I am taking away from all the polls and comments is that women want to vote for other women who reflect their own life experiences and—perhaps a bit chillingly—are suspicious of a woman who has opted to follow a path too far departed from the one they themselves have chosen. And they are particularly unforgiving of a candidate who would go so far as to disparage the lifestyle they themselves have chosen: it's my contention that Clinton has never really been forgiven in some quarters for the "cookie" comment. It lost her the support of women who actually *had* stayed home and baked cookies—and enjoyed doing it.

On the other hand, Palin made no such gaffe and moderately or highly educated women still did not vote for her in large enough numbers. Why? As a senior Democratic operative told me, reflecting on her memories of the day McCain announced he'd added Palin to his team:

> Some of us thought, greatest move in the world for us. Some of us thought, greatest move in the world for them. I said, "We are in trouble here." What Sarah Palin was able to do in that convention was beat the crap out of Barack Obama and still look like a warm, funny mother—a working mom. Someone a hard core Democrat like me could relate to. I didn't agree with her on the issues, but what a great political candidate.

The question comes down to: What are the qualities the next female candidate for president or vice president will need to embody in order either to reflect most broadly the common life experience of women—or to transcend it in a way that is acceptable or appealing to the majority of women? Perhaps as critically, what models do we have for networks that can support these women candidates—from organizing within our local communities to the ultimate position of power: the presidency? Let's face it: by the year 2012, given the trend toward younger voters and, in consequence, younger candidates, baby boomer women of Clinton's generation will probably have passed the time when the first woman president will come from among their numbers. Who will it be instead? And what model can replace the traditional political mechanisms of the women's movement (which were unsuccessful in getting a woman elected)?

Intriguing questions, of course. But, before we get to the answers, let's take a look at one more woman in the 2008 political mix, a now-powerful woman in her own right, Michelle Obama. Perhaps looking at the very traditional role of first lady, and how Mrs. Obama is managing that role, will help us see some of the roadblocks the next woman who is nominated for the presidency will have to overcome.

6

LADIES FIRST

---

*A*MERICA'S FIRST FIRST LADY, Martha Washington, once described her role as being more like that of "a state prisoner than anything else, there is [*sic*] certain bounds set for me which I must not depart from."

We don't know very much about Martha Washington. Most of her letters to her husband—and his to her—were burned, as was often done in the late eighteenth century. But from what we do know, she was an extremely private person, well separated from her husband's public business.

In the more than two hundred years that have passed since the time she wrote those words, the wives of men we have elected to the office of president have all put their own cast on the job of being "first lady." Some, like Jacqueline Kennedy, have been universally beloved. Others, like "Lemonade Lucy" Hayes, have come across as odd historical figures. And some, like Eleanor Roosevelt, have been visible partisan champions for causes that have both polarized the electorate and, likely as not, caused headaches for their husbands as often as they have generated positive press.

None of them have yet written the definitive guide for doing the job, one they entered by virtue of no other qualification than marriage. The title brings with it a good deal of power and, in

---

modern times, staff and offices in the East or even the West Wing of the White House. But, as we can see from Mrs. Washington's letter, the job is not always an easy one. The responsibility of the first lady is traditionally to be the nation's hostess, to run the White House, at least officially, and to entertain visiting dignitaries and their families. The role of hostess presents so little challenge that it has been performed by daughters and others, as was the case in 1856, when James Buchanan, the "bachelor president," took office, enlisting his niece Harriet Lane to serve as the nation's hostess.

The first president's wife to actually be called "first lady," a title coined by the now-defunct *New York Herald,* was Mary Todd Lincoln. The *Herald,* among the most invasive and sensationalist of all the New York newspapers of the time, likely did not mean it as a compliment.

The term didn't really catch on until 1877, when "Lemonade Lucy" Hayes, wife of the nineteenth president, became the first presidential spouse to have graduated from college, and it was used more to honor that accomplishment than to identify her as the president's wife.

Still, the name stuck. From Grace Coolidge, whose grief at the sudden death of her sixteen-year-old son did not keep her from being a most generous and admired first lady (of her role in history Mrs. Coolidge wrote, "I, and yet, not I—this was the wife of the President of the United States and she took precedence over me"), to Eleanor Roosevelt, who became the eyes and ears of her husband, going where his polio would not allow him to go and reporting back, to Jackie Kennedy, who shied away from the term "first lady" because it reminded her of what one might call a race horse, each president's wife has changed the office to suit her own times and her own style—and, more importantly, her husband's style and agenda.

In essence, the job is what each occupant chooses to make of it. The job of first lady brings with it a powerful bully pulpit for those women who have chosen to use it. So, perhaps the experiences of our first ladies can shed some light on what Americans expect from women in positions of power. What do the wives of presidents say about how we expect women to lead?

While only an eight-year slice of a much longer national career, Hillary Clinton's years as first lady certainly provided the jumping-off point for her own bid for elective office. The position gave her the state and national political contacts necessary to muscle Democrat Daniel Patrick Moynihan out of the way so she could run for the Senate in New York. And it helped her build a national network of supporters and donors to fund her political ambitions. But during the 1992 presidential campaign, as was indeed the case during her years as the first lady of Arkansas, she was just as much a lightning rod and a liability as she was an asset.

Consider the "cookie" remark she made about her own career ambitions, which was, to be charitable, ill considered. As I've already said, it has certainly hung around to haunt her, having such an impact on her subsequent career the story bears fuller consideration.

Cyndi Allison, a blogger on the site Suite 101, explains in an April 7, 2008, blog post entitled, "Hillary Clinton Hates Cookie Moms":

> Today I read that Hillary Clinton is slipping bad in North Carolina. It's not likely that she'll take the Tarheel State. I'd be inclined to vote Democrat and also would vote female with a solid candidate that I could trust. I don't trust Hillary though, and she won't be getting my vote. I've had issues with Hillary dating back sixteen years. She's caught some heat for lying lately. Back in the day, she may have been more honest but certainly not very endearing. Here is her comment that made me step back and think: This woman is harsh and does not understand regular old people. "I suppose I could have stayed home and baked cookies and had teas, but what I decided to do was to fulfill my profession which I entered before my husband was in public life" [March 26, 1992, *Nightline*]. As a single mother who has worked my butt off and still made time to bake cookies, I take exception to this stray comment by Hillary Clinton. I would think it would sting even more for women who have taken time out to raise

kids full time. There is honor in that—trust me. And what about Chelsea? She's out stumping for her mom now. Chelsea has to try to explain why her mom said they were under sniper fire when they weren't. Hard spot for a kid—and especially one who was not worth the time to bake cookies for.

This "stray remark" certainly set off a firestorm of criticism back in 1992. As is implied by Allison's comment, it was widely interpreted as an attack on stay-at-home moms. One of the national women's magazines actually went so far as to hold a contest in which they asked readers to vote on whose cookie recipe—Hillary's or Barbara Bush's—they liked better: Hillary's recipe won.

But Clinton's problems went deeper than that. Her husband's suggestion that his campaign slogan might better be expressed as "Buy one, get one free" elevated her in the minds of the electorate, particularly where Clinton critics were concerned. To them, it only amplified the dangers inherent in her image as an elitist ultrafeminist who would be advising on policy inside the White House. It made her a target for the opposition, a legitimate target. And she was not prepared to deal with the fallout.

That may have been the first—but was certainly not the last—time Bill Clinton's penchant for off-the-cuff remarks created problems for Hillary.

Conservative loathing of Hillary Clinton, wrote Jonathan Chait in the *Los Angeles Times* during her presidential campaign, "seems a lot less irrational. We're not frothing Clinton haters like . . . well, name pretty much any conservative. We just really wish they'd go away." He wonders: "Were the conservatives right about Bill Clinton all along?" That is, "right about the Clintons' essential nature?"

As Rich Lowry and Kate O'Beirne wrote for *National Review* in February 2008, Hillary "has used Bill as an obvious crutch, weakening her own image and saddling herself with him for the rest of the campaign, while her feminist allies have made it clear they will do all they can to define her candidacy as an exercise in vintage 1970s-style feminism."

And the former president's usefulness came to an abrupt end during the South Carolina primary, when his ill-considered remarks about Jesse Jackson and Barack Obama alienated the state's all-important bloc of black Democrats.

But what of our nation's next first lady, Laura Welch Bush? She too was an accomplished professional woman when she married her husband. A graduate of Southern Methodist University, Mrs. Bush held a master's degree in library science from the University of Texas at Austin and was employed as a librarian when she met George Walker Bush, married him, and took up political life almost immediately with her husband's run for the U.S. Congress.

It took some time, sixteen years, to be precise, but she eventually became first lady of Texas and then first lady of the United States. When her husband left office, Laura Bush held the distinction of being one of the country's most popular presidential spouses, as measured by modern polling techniques. What was it that made her—and kept her—so beloved by the country?

Was it that she almost ardently distanced herself from any visible policy-making role? Or was it that, while she did give up her own career to advance her husband's, she seemed to relinquish it more willingly, and one might even say more gracefully, than Clinton had?

Or—and here's the real money question—was it that Mrs. Bush was able to seamlessly blend her professional interests with her new national platform? One can hardly say that Mrs. Bush abandoned her own interests to be the nation's hostess when it was those same interests she promoted and advanced with such success in her role as political spouse. These interests included establishing the Texas Book Festival, to raise money for public libraries, and the first lady's Family Literacy Initiative, which encouraged families to read together, while her husband was the governor of Texas. As first lady of the United States, she expanded those interests in promote reading and education, partnering with the Library of Congress to launch the annual National Book Festival.

She also focused intensely on some pretty hard-core women's issues—and I'm not talking about those issues that militant feminists would have you believe were at the forefront of women's concerns, but really basic critical health issues. She served as honorary ambassador to the Heart Truth program to raise awareness about heart disease in women and how to prevent the condition. She became a breast cancer activist when her own mother was diagnosed with breast cancer through her involvement with the group Susan G. Komen for the Cure. She became the first person other than a president to deliver the weekly presidential radio address, speaking passionately about the plight of women in Afghanistan during the ongoing conflict: "The brutal oppression of women is a central goal of the terrorists." In May 2002 she even addressed a speech directly to the people of Afghanistan through Radio Free Europe/ Radio Liberty, a U.S. government broadcasting venture headquartered in Prague.

Her only real venture into policy was in 2005. While Mrs. Bush was on a trip to South Africa, Justice Sandra Day O'Connor announced that she would be resigning from the Supreme Court. Mrs. Bush telephoned her husband to suggest that Justice O'Connor should be replaced by another woman. This helped to lead then-President Bush to ask Harriet Miers to replace O'Connor. When Miers's nomination met with intense criticism due to her less than stellar qualifications, Mrs. Bush leveled charges of sexism at the critics. Though other commentators, and even conservative ones, disagreed with Mrs. Bush—William Kristol of the *Weekly Standard* called it "obviously ridiculous"—I think credit needs to given to Laura Bush for calling it as she saw it—and for being among the first of the conservative women to pick up on the subtle signs that there may indeed be something to this sexism thing after all.

This may be one of Laura Bush's most important lessons for women who have entered—or are thinking about entering—political life. The dignity with which she conducted herself in her role allowed her to be in a position to point out sexism when she saw it. She did her own job so admirably that no one saw it as militant or worse, whining, when she pointed it out—she was conveying the facts as she saw them and her own poise and competence gave her the credibility to make the case. Does calling out sexism make Laura Bush a feminist? If it does, it makes the word—the label—a little less obnoxious. And, apparently, it makes it a little more acceptable as well—Mrs. Bush left the White House with an approval rating of 76 percent. Not bad for a political woman who'd just spent eight years as a tireless advocate for women's issues.

So that brings us to today. What are our expectations for the first lady now? Jump forward sixteen years, from the time Clinton was "running" for the position of first lady, to the 2008 campaign in which Michelle Obama, like Hillary an Ivy League–educated lawyer, a professional and a mom, was looking more and more as if she were going to be the next first lady—and, as an African American woman, a pathbreaking one at that.

It appeared that Obama and his wife had learned well from the Clintons' adventures in campaigning. Never did Obama promise that, in electing him, the nation would also benefit from the brain power of his high-powered wife—a "two for one deal," in the words of Bill Clinton. As first lady, Michelle Obama goes out of her way to distance herself from any apparent involvement in policy making—going so far as to portray herself as just another wife hiding the credit card bills from her husband.

Yet from the get-go, her seemingly innocuous—some would say down-right admirable—comments that she intended to put her young daughters first drew fire.

Regardless, she has actively taken charge of her image. As the *New York Times* has reported, Mrs. Obama "pointedly control[s] her look on the covers of *People, Essence, More* and *O,* Oprah Winfrey's magazine. Editors at *Essence,* who suggested colors, styles and accessories, said her staff did not call to acknowledge their overtures. Editors at *More* said they were dumbfounded when, after painstaking negotiations, Mrs. Obama showed up at the photo shoot with a different dress from the one she had promised to wear. (She ultimately agreed to go back to her first choice, a pink Maria Pinto sheath.)"

"'We were like, 'Excuse me, we tell you what to wear,'" *More* editor-in-chief Lesley Jane Seymour told the *Times,* which went on to report that Mrs. Obama "refused to wear anything other than her own clothes for their October cover. 'She wanted none of that. She was creating the cover. She was creating the image. There's definitely a will of steel there.'"[1]

Said one pundit in the *Boston Globe:*

> However politically strategic and privately compelling, Obama's decision to be foremost the "first mom" potentially sends a wrong message: that high-level paid work and motherhood don't mix, or that women need to be the ones to step down to care for family. . . . The point is, Michelle Obama has been a highly successful working mother and will be again some day. To hear her try to distance herself now from that role does a disservice to our children—and to our country.[2]

Of course, Michelle Obama has also received her share of praise for her decision to focus on her family, and that can't be overlooked. But to question a mother's decision to stay home with her children, a mother who has not been elected to anything, as a disservice to our country? Between Clinton's "cookie" comment and Michelle Obama's desire to be known as the first mom we have to wonder if American women have painted themselves into some sort of corner—a "damned if you do and damned if you don't" impasse on the acceptable way to serve as first lady. It's fair to ask: What's going on here?

It often seems that women in positions of indirect power, where they have no formal role but obviously provide advice and counsel to those who do, put themselves in somebody's line of fire no matter how they choose to handle the influence that comes to them from their husbands' political victories. This is true both in the United States and abroad.

Take Cherie Booth Blair, the most controversial spouse of a British prime minister in recent memory. Educated at the London School of Economics, and a practicing barrister as well as, since 1999, a recorder (permanent, part-time judge) in both the

Country Court and the Crown Court, she often caused heads to shake as she blurred the lines between the legal practice she refused to give up upon her husband's election as prime minister and her more social (and political) duties as the prime minister's wife.

She participated in some very high-profile legal cases—including, currently, the $50 billion prosecution of the Royal Bank of Scotland—received awards, including the Eleanor Roosevelt Val-Kill medal in recognition of her high ideals and courage, and is a patron of many charities, including Breast Cancer Care of the United Kingdom. She is, however, perhaps best remembered in our collective imagination as a New Age sort of person who wears "magic pendants" around her neck and drags her husband to Mexico to participate in a "rebirthing" ritual that involves smearing mud and fruit over each other's bodies.

Or think of France's Carla Bruni Sarkozy, a successful model, an artist, a singer, and a mother. As first lady she is interested in working to end poverty, but the scandals for which she is much better known are on a scale that would have derailed any romance with an American president: her out-of-wedlock child, a child she had with a man named Raphael Enthoven after she ended her affair with Enthoven's father, and the 10,000 shopping bags an outfit named Pardon is producing bearing a nude photo Bruni had posed for in her youth as a supermodel, her crossed hands discreetly covering her body.

Bruni has been so far well received within the international community, if mostly for her fashion sense; but somehow we must assume that the 10,000 nude photos of her are going to have a negative impact, even in sexually liberal France, on her ability to carry out even a nonpolitical, charitable agenda.

America's Michelle Obama, like Cheri Booth Blair and Carla Bruni Sarkozy, is a woman stretching the boundaries of a traditional woman's roles—and all of these women generate both tremendous praise and, quite often, tremendous criticism. Though they act upon the world stage, they are in many ways simply playing out in a larger forum the shift in the roles ordinary woman struggle with the world over.

If they have each brought something unique to the role of first lady, perhaps that is in part, as I mentioned earlier, because it's so undefined. As Anita McBride, chief of staff to Laura Bush, told ABC News, "At the end of the day, this is the most incredible, unique position in our country. . . . It has no job description, no salary, yet an automatically powerful platform from which a president's wife can talk about anything that she cares about—and people will pay attention."[3]

First ladies and the agendas they set for themselves have run the gamut. Some, like Bruni, have been regaled for their glamorous taste and fashion sense. Some, like Grace Coolidge, made it clear that their families came first. And some, like Mamie Eisenhower, have stayed in the background and out of the way.

Still others have operated in "traditional" spheres of influence that followed the pattern set down by Jackie Kennedy, to concern themselves with the nation's art, literature, and culture and to facilitate major beautification and historic renovation efforts. Others have chosen to exert influence over noncontroversial policy or advocacy work that has personal meaning to them, such as Laura Bush's focus on education and the literacy skills of young children, or Nancy Reagan's "Just Say 'No'" anti-drug campaign. Of course, many have combined these facets, and most successfully, but it was not until Hillary Rodham Clinton that a first lady was given such a high-profile formal role as a policymaker and official presidential advisor.

For this, Clinton subjected herself to harsh criticism. But, unlike most of her predecessors, she chose to don the armor and enter the arena in an official capacity, the most famous being her effort to organize a government takeover of the nation's health care system.

That attempt, it must be said, failed badly—and helped lead to the first all-Republican Congress in two generations. It defined her persona, made her "political poison"—at least until she was needed again—and shaped how she is able to work within a new administration presided over by a president of her own party.

As the *New York Times* reported on March 4, 2009,

> Hillary Rodham Clinton has not participated in any of the White House's planning sessions on health care. . . . Mrs. Clinton's distance from the health care initiative, figuratively and literally—she will be in Brussels on Thursday when Mr. Obama begins his effort to overhaul the system with a high-profile gathering of experts—underscores how the Obama White House is grappling with the cloud that still lingers over the Clinton plan fifteen years after it imploded.

Had Mrs. Clinton harbored hopes in 1992 of a future high elected office—one can assume what one wishes on this account—it's clear she would have been much better served in this effort by defining her role of first lady in more traditional terms. The lesson certainly can't be lost on Mrs. Obama, who is a bright woman. Does Michelle Obama harbor political ambitions for herself? That's anyone's guess, but at this point she seems to be playing all of her cards right.

But, while each first lady brings a different point of view and different strengths to the job, one thing is clear: these women matter. They matter to their fellow citizens, and they matter in terms of how a nation is viewed by the global community, depending on the graciousness of the hospitality at the White House, and the causes to which they choose to commit.

They matter for elections as well. Like it or not, a candidate's spouse is part of the package that is being examined and judged by voters. Let's go back to the August 2008 Gallup poll that asked, "When you are considering which presidential candidate to vote for, how important is the candidate's spouse in your decision?"

Overall, 52 percent of people answered either "very important" or "somewhat important," with Republicans "slightly more likely to say the candidate's spouse matters than are Democrats."[4] One can assume that the reason Republicans invest more importance in a candidate's spouse is because they are the party more committed to traditional family values, so the members of the potential first family would make a difference to them. It's not unreasonable to say that in 2008, American voters were, in some way, making up their minds about John McCain and Barack Obama based, at least in part, on what they thought of Cindy McCain and Michelle Obama.

It is also true that a potential first lady's convention speech can have a huge impact on how voters cast their ballots. As the *Washington Post* reported, in 1992,

> Hillary Rodham Clinton took the stage in New York with a 45 percent favorable rating, according to a Gallup-CNN-USA Today poll. Thirty percent held unfavorable impressions of her. After her speech, that initial fifteen point net positive rating increased to a twenty-seven point advantage. Similarly, Elizabeth Dole's 1996 convention speech, delivered in a talk-show style without a podium, boosted her already-positive ratings from 51 percent to 58 percent in post-convention Gallup polling.[5]

And, though Laura Bush had previously told her husband that she would not be persuaded to address the GOP convention in 2000, at which he would be nominated for president, in the end she delivered a keynote address to the delegates to great acclaim.

Throughout the 2008 campaign, both Cindy McCain and Michelle Obama were about equally known and liked by the American public overall. According to Gallup, in early September 2008 (immediately after both conventions), 54 percent of people surveyed held a favorable view of Michelle Obama, while 30 percent held an unfavorable view and 14 percent had no opinion. Similarly, in that same survey period, 51 percent held a favorable view of Cindy McCain, 24 percent had an unfavorable view, and 21 percent had no opinion.[6]

Mrs. McCain, in her 2008 speech at the Republican National Convention, was quick to establish her maternal credentials first. She opened in this way: "John and I are so proud of [our family] and so happy to have them here with us tonight. Nothing has made me happier or more fulfilled in my life than being a mother."

Solidly placing herself in a context of helping, and underpinning it with references to Hurricane Gustav which was, at the time, threatening devastation, she went on:

> But while John and I take great joy in having been able to spend time together this week as a family, our hearts go out to the thousands of families who have had to leave their homes once again due to devastating weather. It is not only our natural instinct to rally to them, to lift them up with our prayers and come to their aid. It is also our duty to our country. That duty is what brings me before you tonight. And it's much larger and more important than just me or John or any of us: It's the work of this great country calling us together, and there is no greater duty than that, no more essential task for our generation right now.

While Mrs. McCain focused on motherhood, prayer, and duty to country, Michele Obama focused on some high-minded political rhetoric, telling a crowd at a speech she gave at the University of California, Los Angeles: "Barack Obama will require you to work. He is going to demand that you shed your cynicism. That you put down your divisions. That you come out of your isolation, that you move out of your comfort zones. That you push yourselves to be better. And that you engage. Barack will never allow you to go back to your lives as usual, uninvolved, uninformed." While some found this kind of talk a bit creepy, even authoritarian—was cynicism going to be criminalized?—it also appears that it was effective.

In fact, in recognition of their popularity as well as their influence, candidates' wives stumped for their husbands' campaigns, often appearing in key battleground states. As the *New York Times* reported, "Mrs. Obama is being deployed where it matters most. Since Labor Day, she has spent three days campaigning in Florida and two days each in Indiana, Michigan, North Carolina, Ohio and Pennsylvania, as well as days in other swing states (sometimes two in a day)."[7]

Not surprisingly, then, the spouses of presidential candidates are closely covered by the media—and that included Bill Clinton during the 2008 presidential primary season. And when they spoke their minds—or got off script—they made news as, for example, when Bill Clinton made his infamous comments about the 2008 South Carolina primary.

As reported in the *Washington Post* by Anne E. Kornblut:

> On Saturday, as Senator Barack Obama was sweeping up the South Carolina primary, former President Bill Clinton was busy downplaying the significance of Obama's impending win, casting it as a function of the state's demographics and the Illinois senator's heavy African American support. "Jesse Jackson won South Carolina in '84 and '88," Clinton said at a rally in Columbia. "Jackson ran a good campaign. And Obama ran a good campaign here." It was a sour note on which to end the contentious Democratic race in South Carolina.[8]

But it is fair to say that describing the comment as a "sour note" was an understatement. It ignited a firestorm of implication that the Clintons were not above race-baiting. And it served to fuel speculation that, as happens to many patients after heart surgery, the formerly amiable President Clinton, had undergone a personality change that impaired his competence. The great irony, as some see it, is that the first serious woman to be a candidate for a major party's presidential nomination was brought down by the incompetence of two men: her husband, a former president, and Mark Penn, her campaign manager.

Similarly, it was when Michelle Obama said on the campaign trail that "for the first time in my adult life I am proud of my country because it feels like hope is finally making a comeback"[9] that the news media—and blogosphere—hopped to attention and jumped all over it.

The crux of the criticism was summarized by *Weekly Standard* editor Bill Kristol, who told FOX News,

> She was an adult when we won the Cold War without firing a shot. She was an adult for the last twenty-five years of economic progress, social progress . . . I think the Democrats have to be careful . . . they're running against the status quo. . . . You have to be careful not to let that slide into a kind of indictment of America. Because I don't think the American people think on the

whole that the last twenty-five years of American history is a narrative of despair and nothing to be proud of.[10]

The Obama campaign tried to walk back Mrs. Obama's comment (which is never a good sign), by saying:

> Of course Michelle is proud of her country, which is why she and Barack talk constantly about how their story wouldn't be possible in any other nation on Earth. What she meant is that she's really proud at this moment because for the first time in a long time, thousands of Americans who've never participated in politics before are coming out in record numbers to build a grass-roots movement for change.[11]

Mrs. Obama herself edited the sentiment in subsequent campaign speeches: "For the first time in my adult lifetime, I'm really proud of my country," she now explained, " . . . not just because Barack has done well, but because I think people are hungry for change. I have been desperate to see our country moving in that direction and just not feeling so alone in my frustration and disappointment."[12]

The reaction was reminiscent of the flap over Hillary Clinton's "baking cookies" remark in 1992, or her claim that same year to *60 Minutes* that she "wasn't some little woman 'standing by my man' like Tammy Wynette." It was a culturally dismissive remark that left many Tammy Wynette fans—and others—smarting, another casual remark that has served to continue to define her.

And there were many who weren't any more ready to let Michele Obama off the hook either. "Can it really be there has not been a moment during that time when she felt proud of her country," went an article in *Commentary* magazine. "Forget matters like the victory in the Cold War; how about only things that have made liberals proud—all the accomplishments of inclusion? How about the passage of the Civil Rights Act of 1991? Or Ruth Bader Ginsburg's elevation to the Supreme Court?"

Among others, first lady Laura Bush came to Michelle Obama's defense, saying that "I think she probably meant 'I'm more proud.' That's what she really meant. . . . You have to be really careful in what you say because everything you say is looked at and in many cases misconstrued."[13]

Indeed, the scrutiny on the campaign trail is intense, as Mrs. Bush would well know. But however Mrs. Obama's comments might have been misconstrued, as Mrs. Bush suggests, the reaction to them, in this case, demonstrates the glass house the candidate's wives—and husbands—necessarily live in when their spouses pursue public office.

That scrutiny is applied not only to the candidate's spouse, but to his or her extended family. Ronald and Nancy Reagan's relations with their children—including those from his first marriage to Jane Wyman—were tabloid fodder for years. And the Bush twins, Jenna and Barbara, were a source of repeated embarrassment to their parents throughout their first year in the White House, though it can be argued they were simply behaving like what today passes for normal young ladies of college age. Chelsea Clinton did manage to remain out of the spotlight in the years before she headed off to college, but that was only because of the iron-fisted retribution the Clintons threatened to bring down on any publication or news organization that decided to focus their attentions on her.

The 2008 campaign was little different from those in years past. The children of the Republican candidates in particular came in for a great deal of attention. Compellingly, in my judgment, much of that revealed a sexist and ageist framework.

During the 2008 presidential campaign, Meghan McCain, John and Cindy McCain's twenty-three-year-old daughter, began blogging. She set up her McCainBlogette.com site in support of her father's candidacy, to help him attract the younger voters who were having trouble connecting with him. Well, while her dad might have difficulty connecting to them, she herself—as evidenced from her well-traveled site and her increasing media exposure—is popular with young voters her own age. She is still quite young, but her posts are for the most part clever, well thought out, and full of pride in her Republican roots.

Like many of her generation, she is more moderate on the social issues that form one of the pillars of Republican philosophy; she has the raw potential to aid the party in terms of attracting the young people it now so sorely lacks—although McCain, who is an active participant in the Twitter social media network, seems to relish controversy.

Here's one analysis, courtesy of the *Washington Post*'s Kathleen Parker, on March 25, 2009:

> Young McCain . . . recently made waves at The Daily Beast when she picked a fight with conservative media mavens Ann Coulter and Laura Ingraham. This is enough sport to make the little dog laugh, to say nothing of the dish and the spoon. McCain, just twenty-four, is one smart cookie. In a matter of weeks she has created a brand, presenting herself as a fresh face of her daddy's party and a voice for young conservatives. Strategically speaking, what better way to launch herself than to challenge the reigning diva herself, Miz Coulter? Madonna, meet Britney.

My reaction to this sort of coverage is to shake my head and say, "Not again!"

While the jury is still out on Miss McCain—she is just launching her career and has a lot to learn—here, again, is a young woman who has undeniably experienced the political process in a way few young people are privileged to do, and is one sassy social media maven to boot, but the media are reducing any credibility she might have by comparing her to Britney Spears. I have to wonder, if Miss McCain were John McCain's son and trying to take on the concerns of young Republicans in a way that is serious and thoughtful, would the press reduce a young man by referring to him as Zac Efron or another reigning teen idol?

Not all of the verbal abuse Miss McCain now has to deal with is coming from the media. Some is coming from within her own party. It was Ingraham who, in responding to one of Miss McCain's reasoned blogs, parodied the younger McCain on her radio show in Valley-girlese: "Okay, I was really hoping that I was going to get that role in *The Real World,* but then I realized that, well, they don't like plus-sized models."

Instead of returning Miss McCain's reasoned argument with a reasoned response, Ingraham attacked her weight and body image. I can't put it any more plainly than this: we women cannot expect men to look beyond our gender and our physical attributes and focus on our input and ideas on the issues if we do not refrain from making sexist attacks on each other.

Additionally, we have to ask ourselves how wise it is for Republicans to try to discredit a young woman who has a growing following among other young people. If the Republican Party hopes to expand its tent, McCain could well be a voice to attract these young people to the conservative principles she espouses. After all, as Parker pointed out in summing up her *Post* article: "Who better to [do that] than a young maverick named McCain?" It is the job of more seasoned Republicans to mentor this young woman and strategically develop her talents, which will allow her to become the asset to the party she so clearly desires to be.

So, we know that it is really a candidate's entire family who influences how people vote. But let's get back to the main topic of this chapter: What do we want, or even expect, from our leader's spouse? It's a fair question, but the answer is not necessarily clear. What qualities would make an ideal American first lady?

In 2004 Gallup asked Americans "who they think better fits their idea of what a first lady should be, Laura Bush or Hillary Rodham Clinton?" In response, 52 percent chose Laura Bush and 43 percent Hillary Clinton; the other 5 percent picked both, neither, or had no opinion.[14] It's hard to say how significant this nine-point gap really is; after all, there is a three-point margin of error, and the question was asked during President Bush's term. And, not surprisingly, Republicans surveyed overwhelmingly chose Laura Bush and Democrats chose Hillary Clinton while independents were split—51 percent for Bush, 42 percent for Clinton.

Interestingly, Hillary Clinton was preferred by eighteen- to twenty-nine-year-olds (62 percent to 35 percent), while Laura Bush came out ahead among all age groups over thirty. The differences by gender were less distinct: "55 percent of men say Laura Bush best fits their idea of a first lady, while 40 percent believe Clinton does. Among women . . . 50 percent [say] Bush is the better fit, and 45 percent [say] Clinton is."[15]

It's perhaps not surprising that Laura Bush bested Hillary Clinton in a head-to-head poll. She was consistently popular (with Republicans and Democrats alike) throughout her husband's two terms in office, including when his own approval ratings were at their lowest. When the Bushes left office, Laura Bush's favorability rating—at 76 percent—was nearly double her husband's 40 percent.[16]

By contrast, Hillary Clinton's "personal high favorable rating of 67 percent is just slightly better than Bush's *lowest* favorable rating of 63 percent." The survey also points out that just before George H. W. Bush left the White House in January 1993, his wife Barbara enjoyed an 85 percent favorable opinion rating.[17]

It seems pretty clear that at least part of the reason Laura Bush was so popular is that she was not associated with the unpopular policies of her husband's administration—in the way that Hillary Clinton was associated with negative events and policies of the Clinton administration. Mrs. Bush was by no means squirreled away, and she did at times publicly defend her husband and his administration but, in general, the causes that she championed—children's literacy and education, for example, as well as women's rights and HIV/AIDS and malaria awareness abroad—are unquestionably important to our nation and the world, but they are not in any way controversial.

On the other hand, as first lady, Hillary Clinton was in the public eye, both in the more conventional first lady roles—representing the United States abroad, advocating causes—but also in a much more unconventional and pathbreaking role—as a key member of her husband's policy team, at least at the beginning of his first term.

It was no surprise that she took such an active policy role. She was sold to the American people this way—and perhaps justifiably so given her own background and career achievements. Just by virtue of being different, this would have been controversial, as many groundbreaking events often are. But throw in her leadership of President Clinton's massive effort to reform health care during his first term—the President's Task Force on National Health Care Reform—in 1993–1994 and the very public failure of that effort.

Add this to the environment of constant scandal—from Whitewater to Lewinsky—that swirled through Clinton's two terms, as well as the intense partisanship (from both the White House and Capitol Hill) that surrounded the Clinton White House. Given all of these factors, it adds up to a very polarized view of Hillary Clinton as first lady of the United States.

Many applauded her leadership on international women's issues and her involvement in policy—including health care reform, even though she was ultimately unsuccessful with that initiative. Indeed, in late 1993 and early 1994, her favorability numbers were still in the high fifties, as were her husband's. But her unfavorable numbers have always been stubbornly high as well—hovering in the thirties and forties, and even as high as 50 percent, throughout her time as first lady.[18]

Hillary Clinton and Laura Bush offer two clear-cut and opposing models of leadership for a first lady. There were some similarities, of course, but also some marked, very public differences. It is conceivable that the space in between offers an opening for a new model of first lady—one that Michelle Obama seems a natural to fill.

You can't be all things to all people, or so the saying goes. But if anyone in the United States is expected to try, it is the first lady. And, even in her brief tenure as first lady so far, Michelle Obama is learning this quickly—and seems to be embracing it with relative ease. As if being the nation's first African American first lady isn't groundbreaking enough, Michelle Obama appears to have an opening to shape a new model for this traditional role, much in the way that her husband has rocked the political landscape.

On the campaign trail, there were continuous musings in the press about what "type" of first lady Michelle Obama would be. As has been mentioned, she has referred to herself as "mom-in-chief," and said, "My girls are the first thing I think about when I wake up in the morning and the last thing I think about when I go to bed. When people ask me how I'm doing, I say, 'I'm only as good as my most sad child.'"[19] Initially, this type of comment drew some fire—inciting overwrought panic among a certain segment of feminists that as first lady Michelle Obama would be too traditional.

Such an idea—that she would be setting some sort of "bad example" by putting her own career on hold to care for the couple's children, help them adjust and keep them grounded, as her husband stepped into the most high-profile, high-pressure job in the world—is laughable. And moreover, it's hard to imagine how we could possibly fault her—or any parent—for putting the needs of her children first.

During the campaign, the Obama team made little secret of how Michelle envisioned herself as first lady. According to the *New York Times,* "Obama advisers say, Mrs. Obama would focus first on her family and then on the issues facing women and military spouses as those groups deal with the economic crisis and the return of troops from Iraq. She also plans to take up national service as an issue, aides say. She will not have a major policy role, they are quick to add, and does not plan to have an office in the West Wing."[20]

Similarly, in June 2008, Mrs. Obama told the co-hosts of *The View* that she was "taking some cues from" Laura Bush, adding that "there's a reason people like her—it's because she doesn't, sort of, you know, add fuel to the fire."[21] And, at least based on her start as first lady, she seems to be sticking with that game plan, placing a particular focus on military families and also work-life issues (a natural for the nation's most high-profile working mom).

As ABC's Cokie Roberts put it, "I think Mrs. Obama wants to make it clear that she puts her children first and that she understands the plight of other mothers who are trying to do the balancing act."

In her first months as first lady, Michelle Obama, among other things, opened up the White House kitchen to journalists (and a few lucky culinary students) before the president's annual dinner with the nation's governors; visited various cabinet-level departments to address federal employees; invited two hundred schoolchildren to the White House to celebrate African American history month; spent time with members of the military and their families at Fort Bragg in North Carolina; and visited nonprofit organizations in Washington, D.C. And, of course, she accompanied her two young daughters to school each day and, along with her husband, attended their parent-teacher conferences.

At the same time, though, she has not shied away from defending her husband's administration and policies. While she may not have "a major policy role," she is certainly an effective saleswoman.

In her remarks to employees at the Department of Housing and Urban Development (HUD) in early February, Michelle Obama talked about home ownership and the president's economic stimulus package, in addition to praising and thanking federal employees, which was ostensibly the reason for her trip to HUD. She said,

> It's of critical importance that we stem the tide of foreclosures and find a way to keep people in their homes. . . . Homeownership, at least as I knew it growing up on the South Side of Chicago, has always been one of the building blocks for strong neighborhoods, for strong schools and for strong families. People who own their homes and take care of their homes, it leads to the well-being of the entire community. . . . [HUD] is going to play a critical role in implementing elements of the Economic Recovery and Reinvestment Plan that will help our communities.[22]

It is not at all surprising to me that Michelle Obama would emerge as an effective voice for her husband's administration. After all, as has been mentioned, she was popular on the campaign trail—and with the press—and has high approval ratings from the American people. It seems to me that by positioning herself as an advocate for the Obama administration's policies, but not as a member of the team *developing* those policies (if that's what she continues to do), she has the potential to be an effective sales-woman who doesn't get a whole lot of scrutiny, at least politically or from a policy perspective. If she plays her cards right, she will indeed, like Laura Bush, be the embodiment of a strong woman supporting her family, as well as being an effective working mom who endorses the national policies of importance to her.

Ironically, as Hilary Rosen stated to me, Michele Obama may have Hillary Clinton to thank for that.

> When, really, by all accounts, [Clinton] found her voice was when she connected with not having to be one kind of woman but being what we all have to be, which is many kinds of women. We have to be professionals. We have to be moms. We have to be wives. We have to be the organizer of the family's business and the choice-maker of financial decisions. . . . In essence, where Hillary ended up going in the spring, connecting all the dots of being a woman and being a candidate. . . . It clearly created a path and a beacon for women going forward. Maybe the biggest example of that is Michelle Obama. She didn't have to prove she was smart. People accepted she was smart. She just had to be who she was.[23]

Who could have predicted, just a year ago, that Hillary Clinton would be Michelle Obama's biggest benefactor?

But there's certainly one area where Mrs. Obama will continue to be heavily scrutinized. Even while she's been making the rounds in Washington, Michelle Obama has been closely watched by one group above all others—the fashionistas.

The coverage of Michelle Obama's wardrobe choices and of her super-toned arms has been exhaustive (and exhausting). However, tiring as it is to talk about, it is the one place where Mrs. Obama is in danger of making some missteps: Mrs. Obama has a propensity for sleeveless dresses and blouses—she even wore a sleeveless in her official White House portrait photo, released on February 27, 2009. Moreover, the clothing she chooses—notably the bright red dress she wore to meet the Bushes and receive her first tour of the White House prior to her husband's inauguration—fits a bit snugly.

While Mrs. Obama can carry off these sorts of fashions, she risks allowing her fashion choices to overshadow the substance of her mission and advocacy.

Consider *New York Times* columnist David Brooks's snarky comment about our first lady's biceps? This knowledge comes to us courtesy of his colleague Maureen Dowd, who wrote about a conversation she had with him:

"When I asked David Brooks about her amazing arms, he indicated it was time for her to cover up. 'She's made her point,' he said. 'Now she should put away Thunder and Lightning.'"[24]

Criticism of her wardrobe and style notwithstanding, Michelle Obama seems to be embracing a "middle ground" in terms of how she's handling her new job. Call it a new model or just Michelle Obama's take on the role. She is fulfilling the more conventional duties of the first lady, although giving them her own spin, advocating for issues that she holds close, but also being an important member of her husband's team—maybe not his policymaking team directly, but as one of his most effective, convincing surrogates.

And this is a role that she is not only well suited to—she's certainly proved at least that much—but also one that the American people are likely to embrace, especially considering the fact that we don't seem entirely sure about what we want from our first lady. According to a survey of women taken after the 2008 election, commissioned by Lifetime Networks, when asked to consider their preferred role for Michelle Obama, "49 percent would like to see her get involved in a few issues, while 38 percent say she should focus on being a wife and mother."

The issues that respondents want her to address include traditional areas like education (33 percent) and to some extent work-life balance (22 percent). Interestingly, only 12 percent believe health care should be a focus. Perhaps the aftertaste of another first lady's failed health care reform efforts lingers. Regardless, Mrs. Obama's tremendous popularity and personal experience offer an opportunity to stretch the boundaries of the Office of First Lady even further.[25]

7

WHAT'S NEXT

WE WON THE BATTLES.
WHEN WILL WE WIN THE WAR?

*I*N CASE YOU HAVE begun to despair that the United States is behind the rest of the world in terms of getting a handle on the blight of sexism in politics, please don't.

It's still true that other countries have certainly beat America in electing women to positions of national leadership—but you can rest easy. Though the United Kingdom has indeed enjoyed the strong leadership of the Iron Lady, Margaret Thatcher, it also endures a *Daily Mail* online columnist named Quentin Letts. Letts's column on March 26, 2008, was titled "Oh Yes, Minister! Meet the Women Voted the World's Most Stunning Politicians (what WOULD Sir Humphrey say . . .)."[1]

Well, leaving Sir Humphrey aside (I wasn't sure who he was when I first saw the article either; turns out he's a character from a 1980s British sitcom, *Yes Minister,* of all things), let's look at what Letts had to say: "[H]ow come the French have such knockout lovelies for their female politicians? And how come our Hon Lady Members are, well, a little more on the bookish side?" The column goes on to caption photographs of France's new minister for overseas territories, Christine Kelly ("The thirty-nine-year-old looks like a model out of a lads' mag. . . . French parliamentary sketchwriters get to feast their pens on the pouting, pearly-toothed creation. . . ."), Luciana León, who, at thirty, is Peru's youngest ever congresswoman, and "the sultry" Anna-Maria Galojan of Estonia.

Letts goes on to indict some of Britain's female politicians in such offensive terms I absolutely have to repeat at least one of them here for it to be believed: "[W]e have the likes of . . . the former public schoolgirl who has a cough like a sergeant major and hauls around a handbag which may well contain boulders." It's an international inventory of male chauvinism! Oh no, the United States has, at least from this angle of the problem, no shame to bear.

So what do we do about it? In my view, the 2008 election season did prove that America is ready for a woman in the White House. How do we make the possibility a reality?

While neither Hillary Clinton nor Sarah Palin was victorious, they were contenders—and quite serious ones at that. And while the treatment they endured was at times brutal, they also won some important battles: they raised serious money, they got millions of votes across the nation, they galvanized supporters, and, on some level, they exposed our biases—both publicly and privately held—toward women running for the White House. In so doing, I hope they also made these biases less tolerable for the future.

A nonpartisan poll commissioned by Lifetime Networks after the 2008 election found that by

> a margin of more than 12 to 1, women declared the 2008 election cycle a "step forward" and not a "step backward" toward electing the first female President of the United States. . . . Additionally, 93 percent of women said that the candidacies of Sarah Palin and Hillary Clinton should encourage more women to run for office and 79 percent said their experiences made running for office more appealing.[2]

So when will we see a woman in the White House—serving not as first lady, but as president or vice president? Who will this woman be? And will she be president or vice president? Will it be a woman already serving in national political office—a current member of the House or Senate—or will it be a governor? Will it be a woman who has made a name for herself in the corporate sector?

Will this woman, as Kate Zernike wrote in the *New York Times*, "come from the South, or west of the Mississippi . . . be a Democrat who has won in a red state, or a Republican who has emerged from the private sector to run for governor . . . have executive experience . . . proven herself to be 'a fighter' . . . be young enough to qualify as post feminist . . . [and] be married with children, but not young children"? As Zernike reminds us, "Oh, and she may not exist."[3]

Let's take the optimistic view. Let's say she does exist. Let's look at the possibility that this candidate, four or eight years from now, might well be Sarah Palin.

Plenty of people have written Palin's political obituary, at least for national office, but her own intentions are less clear. The speculation about Palin's political ambitions began even before the 2008 election was lost—in the mainstream media and on the blogs. Politico.com ran a story on October 28, 2008, titled, "Is Sarah Palin preparing for 2012?"[4] Huffington Post's Matt Litman posted "Sarah Palin in 2012? Get Ready For It" on October 8, 2008.[5] There were dozens of others. Many of these stories seemed to sprout more from perceptions of "dissention" or "tension" in the McCain-Palin camp than from Palin's actual intentions, though Palin herself was discreet about any plans she might have throughout the 2008 campaign.

Her discretion, however, didn't stop some reporters from questioning her loyalty to her ticket even during the campaign. In its online column "Trailwatch," *Forbes* magazine dished:

> Political reporters are feasting on a feud between anonymous John McCain and Sarah Palin aides. Some accuse the Governor of Alaska of behaving like a diva and going rogue. Wait, don't

mavericks routinely go rogue? Palin's supporters have responded by accusing the McCain campaign of botching Palin's introduction to the national political scene, perhaps killing off a rising star in the Republican party. Meanwhile, say party insiders (also under the cover of anonymity), Palin is pursuing her own 2012 ambitions at the expense of the current ticket.[6]

It is interesting (if not infuriating) to note not only the condescending tone of *Forbes*'s comments, but the word they chose to refer to Palin: "diva." While there are any number of derogatory words that can be used to refer to strong women, "diva" just happens to be one that can be printed in a family newspaper.

Since the election and her subsequent resignation as Alaska's governor, Palin's discretion and loyalty to the conservative movement remain intact. Whether she'll seek future office is no more certain, however, as she did not make her intentions clear about a 2012 presidential bid in her final resignation speech. She herself told Scott Conroy of CBS News, "'Oh, you know it seems like so far,' she said as she held her six-month-old son Trig in her arms. '2012, we will be enrolling him in kindergarten.'"[7]

I say we take her at her word for the time being, and this in spite of the fact that she has launched her own political action committee, SarahPAC. While reporters like Sam Stein of the Huffington Post may speculate—"a move meant to secure firmer roots within the Republican community but one that will undoubtedly spur talk of another run for national office"[8]—Palin herself remains circumspect, focused on her family, writing a book, and building a center-right coalition.

Though we can assume that some of the vitriol and polarization that surrounded Sarah Palin's vice presidential candidacy will fade with time, it's an open question if she will remain a frontrunner (or even in the leading pack) with conservatives or, more importantly, with the Republican establishment. According to an ABC News/*Washington Post* poll, in the days leading to her exit from public office, Palin's favorable rating dipped to just 40 percent—the lowest level in ABC News/*Washington Post* polling since she first appeared as Senator John McCain's running mate.[9]

However, as Reihan Salam wrote in the *Atlantic*, "As a rule, conservatives remain enthusiastic about a Palin presidential run, while moderates are opposed. But so far, there is little indication that Palin is preparing the groundwork for a national campaign, with the exception of making campaign appearances in key races, including Georgia Senator Saxby Chambliss's reelection run-off."[10]

But *should* Palin run? John McCain did her no favors in this effort when he was asked that question on *Meet the Press* on March 29, 2009. Not only did he fail to give his former running mate his wholehearted endorsement, he ticked off a laundry list of possible other candidates—all of them, not surprisingly, male—and noted that before he endorsed he'd "have to see who the candidates are and what the situation is at the time."

However, even a quick glance at the Internet—and sites like Palin4pres.com—will tell a different story. Online speculation about a Palin running mate for 2012 is already a hot topic for discussion (Bobby Jindal of Louisiana and Mitt Romney of Massachusetts are currently running in a tie for Palin's number two spot, at 43 percent each, with Michael Steele, the current RNC chairman, at 14 percent, and Tim Pawlenty a distant fourth at 4 percent).

If not Sarah Palin, then who? Well, it's too early to speculate.

There's always Hillary Clinton. But I would have to say it's a long shot that we'll see her run for her party's nomination a second time. Assuming she wouldn't challenge her boss in 2012, what are the realities that would affect the potential of a Clinton campaign in 2016?

First of all, she would be sixty-nine at the time of the election. And her running would assume one of two things: that Obama wins a second term and Vice President Joe Biden decides not to run in 2016, or, if Biden *does* run, that Clinton would choose to challenge an incumbent vice president (in whose administration she served as secretary of state) for the nomination. This seems exceedingly unlikely. Stranger things have happened, but my sense is that politically, once Hillary Clinton became the sixty-seventh U.S. secretary of state, she took herself out of the running to be the first woman president of the United States.

Interestingly, Americans seem quite happy with Hillary Clinton's current position as secretary of state. She and President Obama shared top billing on Gallup's "Most Admired Men and Women of 2008" list. And, in a Gallup poll released in mid-January 2009, 65 percent of Americans had a favorable opinion of Clinton; and 56 percent expected her to be an outstanding or above-average secretary of state.[11]

In a poll of women commissioned by Lifetime Networks and conducted after the election, 58 percent said that they would prefer Clinton to be secretary of state, 18 percent would prefer her to be president, and 18 percent said neither.[12]

Perhaps we should look around a little more broadly, outside the current halls of political power, as we cast about for potential candidates. What about an executive—like former eBay CEO Meg Whitman of California? Whitman—or a woman like her—would seem a possibility for eventually reaching the highest office in the land. With her leadership of eBay she's established her street cred as an experienced executive—according to *Forbes,* she helped "grow the company from a fledging $4.7 million (sales) auction Web site into an $8 billion online behemoth" before she stepped down as CEO in March 2008.[13] This is an obvious plus with the economy in tatters.

With such personal success in the corporate world comes another bonus: personal wealth to devote to one's campaign; *Forbes* estimates Whitman's net worth at $1.3 billion. But, realistically, her future political success becomes possible only after she's run the state of California for a few terms, and she hasn't even been elected governor yet.

Quite wisely, she's launched her 2009 campaign for governor on the idea of creating a "New California" out of the wreckage of the state's current economic and fiscal mess. "Restoring California will not be easy. It will take time to uproot old habits . . . old ways of thinking . . . and old ways of doing business. But do it we can, and do it we must, because we all love California too much to let it fail."[14]

There's another plus, too, to a Whitman presidential candidacy: at least right now, a woman like Meg Whitman doesn't carry the political baggage (and voting record) that, say, a member of Congress (or of a state legislature) would have. That may seem a net negative—what does she stand for?—but it allows her to define her policy positions herself, something she had better do quickly before others do it for her.

Coming from California as a pro-choice Republican with a more moderate stance on gay rights would, some analysts say, also serve her well on the national front because it would allow her to separate herself from the crowded field of white male traditional conservatives who will dominate the next two primary cycles.

Sarah Palin's candidacy would seem to make that point pretty clearly: established women's groups had a field day with Palin because she is pro-life, and that sort of knee-jerk reaction to a candidate would be nipped in the bud with a woman who was more moderate on these hot-button issues. Those moderate views would also help to narrow, or even close, the persistent gender gap that Republican candidates continue to face. This is one of those difficult areas where, though some might not like it or agree with it, the writing appears to be on the wall.

As has been discussed throughout this book, Sarah Palin's ascendancy to the national spotlight made plain a few major truths of our current political environment: that feminists cannot possibly be pro-life is a view widely held among those who claim to lead the women's movement.

As we saw, Palin's own issue positions and beliefs were viewed as so heretical to the rights of women—as defined by women—that they were dismissed out of hand. Palin's views weren't possibly real, just politically expedient. And, in the eyes of many women (who should know better), because of her pro-life position (and for other reasons) Palin did not earn herself the right to run for high office without having to deal with sexist treatment—or at least she hadn't earned the right to be defended with the same indignation that so many applied (quite rightly) to attacks on Hillary Clinton's candidacy.

On a personal level, Meg Whitman is now fifty-two years old and is married—her husband is a neurosurgeon at Stanford University Medical Center—with two college-age sons.[15] It's not suggesting Meg Whitman is going to be president one day—it would be pretty foolish to make such a bold prediction. And, as I said, she's only a candidate for the California Republican party.

However, Whitman represents one plausible *model* for victory. She's got the chops—particularly on economic and financial matters; she's a moderate Republican from a liberal state; she's got a family with (soon-to-be) adult children; and, she's got enough money so that, if she wanted to, she could finance her own campaigns. In other words, she's moving up the "acceptance" curve. And that curve isn't a short one—though she was involved in the presidential campaigns of Mitt Romney and, later, John McCain, her success in the political realm remains to be proven.

The idea of a viable woman presidential candidate coming from the business world also recognizes another reality: the pool of *political* talent is way too small. Or, as Vicki Haddock put it, we face a "lack of women in the political pipeline. The United States ranks 68th among the world's countries in terms of our ratio of female representatives in the national legislature, according to the Inter-Parliamentary Union. That places us far behind top-ranked Rwanda, where roughly half of the legislative seats are held by women, and behind every country in Scandinavia as well as China, Iraq and Afghanistan."[16] Here in America, only seven of our fifty statehouses are occupied by women at present, with two Republican women governors, and four Democratic.

I recognize that some of these assumptions are not traditional or expected. I'm merely examining the world as it is, especially for women seeking to lead. Others may emerge—and, indeed, I think that's very likely. We shall see. But where will these women come from?

We've already seen one woman from the heart of the 1960s and 1970s women's movement make her bid for a major party nomination—and lose. It seems unlikely that another woman from this era of feminism will throw her hat in the ring in 2012 and, especially, in 2016. Even Clinton conceded, during her 2008 run, that when her husband remarked at times that she looked tired, she would remind him that he knew very well how exhausting it was to run for the presidency—and *he* did it when they were both fifteen years younger!

So, if it's unlikely that the next women candidates will come from the Betty Friedan/Gloria Steinem model, where will they emerge from? How can we nurture their talents and foster their entry into political life? On-ramping women to careers in public office or as government or political operatives requires an essential combination of access to opportunities, educational and professional credentials, a record of accomplishment, strong support networks, and a bit of luck. And the process of "learning the ropes" in and around Washington is especially challenging for women who lack strong political ties or financial resources, which is often the case for young women and women of color.

One alliance, specifically comprised of a bipartisan group of African American women leaders, has quietly cultivated its members, personally and professionally, for decades. By mid-2007, potential Democratic presidential contenders competed for their support and counsel.

While some African American women were highly successful during the George W. Bush administration, their political prowess under the Obama administration has expanded.

Seven of about three dozen senior positions on President Obama's team are filled by African American women. As Krissah Thompson wrote in an article titled "The Ties That Align" for the *Washington Post* on March 18, 2009, "Veterans in town see them as part of the steady evolution of power for black women, not only in the White House but also across the country—the business world, in academia, in policy circles."

I think the term "evolution" is particularly appropriate here. Through church affiliations and community involvement they have marked—as Thompson says—"another step in the long journey of black women from outsiders to gatekeepers in political Washington. They have quietly entered their jobs with little attention paid to the fact that they are the largest contingent of high-ranking black women to work for a president."

From Jimmy Carter's appointment of Patricia Roberts Harris to serve as secretary of housing and urban development, thus making her the first black woman in the presidential line of succession, to the contingent of black women who were introduced to national politics during the Reverend Jesse Jackson's failed bids for the Democratic nomination for the presidency in 1984 and 1988—which included Donna Brazile, the first African American woman to direct a major political campaign—these sister-friends have helped each other to their current powerful positions by doing everything from recommending churches and hair salons to giving fashion advice and offering babysitting services.

They have risen up not because they were brash and demanding, but because they worked hard as individuals and helped each other earn their current power.

A bit of my personal story is, I think, relevant here to underscore my point. I first came to Washington, D.C., to forge my career in the early 1990s. In all the years I have lived here there ßhave been many big changes around the city—new administrations, new Congresses convening—but I have noticed one smaller and still significant change: there are now more hair salons catering to the needs of ethnic women, by far, than there were when I got here.

Oh, how we Latinas were trying to fit into this city when I first got here in the 1990s! We were trying to blend into the Washington scene. More than a few Latinas hit the traditional and upscale hair salons of chic D.C. asking for "golden highlights," expecting to look like J-Lo. Instead they came out looking like Mimi from the *Drew Carey Show*. "Who did your hair?" we'd ask each other. "You look so *chola*."

A *chola*, according to the Urban Dictionary, is a

> *firme hyna* (Latina) that wears a lot of makeup: thick eyeliner, liquid eyeliner on top going out of your eye dark brown or red lipstick and eyebrows drawn on or really thin. We mostly have permed hair with hella gel or straight and arched on top. We kick it with people in our own barrio and not really claiming a color mainly your raza.[17]

It was not a compliment.

We wanted to fit in and, instead, all we did was find ways to stand out even more. So we looked around us and tried to find the things that would make us part of the crowd. We cut our hair in short bobs hoping that would make us more like the senators' wives we wanted to emulate. And we looked around at what these women were wearing—St. John suits! We'd find our St. Johns in the off-off-off-designer discount stores and put them on to go about our business. So legions of young women were running around Capitol Hill, trying to look like we belonged there, in clothes that were not just age-inappropriate but unflattering.

We nurtured each other through this time in our lives—and the older ethnic women who mentored us nurtured us, too. We also had male mentors—mostly, perhaps surprisingly, white men. Patti Solis Doyle has shared a lot of life experience with me as a Latina making her way in the brave new world of Washington, and in redefining the role our cultures had dictated to us:

> My mother was born in Monterrey, Mexico. She was brought up, like any woman in Mexico, to be very submissive. When [my parents] emigrated to Chicago that all dropped. They both had to work. She became an equal partner almost. She still did all the cooking and the cleaning. When my father came home he

was served. But she had a strong role in controlling the little money that they had. She was really the hard-ass when it came to the kids, versus my father who was so much more fun-loving. As a result, my family now is a very matriarchal family.

Many of us can speak of similar, shared experiences. Individuals like then–RNC Chairman Jim Nicholson, former congressman Henry Bonilla, and renowned GOP pollster Lance Tarrance Jr. each helped me when I first arrived in Washington fifteen years ago. They encouraged me to remain in politics, cultivate my skills, and expand my networks and created opportunities to grow my business in ways that both challenged me and enhanced my understanding of the way Washington works. When I did not agree with the Republican "establishment," they helped me find my own voice and pathway to add value to a party system I desperately tried to fit into.

Not every experience or opportunity was a positive one, but it didn't need to be. In my time at CNN, more than one Democrat woman told me, sotto voce, about the problems with the "white boys club" they had encountered while working in senior positions on national campaigns.

Being a political neophyte is tough enough. Learning the culture in Washington only adds to that burden, especially when the cultural norms appear contrary to your own.

I'm sure this is an experience that crosses party, ethnic, and educational lines. This knowledge helped me to understand that I was not alone in my perception that some men in the political world, and some other women, find a strong, smart, ambitious woman threatening and distasteful—even in the party that is supposed to be more woman friendly.

But, slowly, through the good advice and wise counsel and warm nurturing people, men and women, friends and families, we learned to navigate the ropes of Washington and make the connections we needed to succeed. We learned the art of our crafts so we could make careers for ourselves. And we learned how to dress and do our hair and wear our makeup so that we looked sharp and what we had to offer was taken seriously.

It's been a long road from those days in the early 1990s to now, and I find quite a contrast in Michelle Obama, who seems to be striking out on her own with rather fearless fashion choices. A cardigan sweater to Buckingham Palace to meet the queen. Going sleeveless at Number 10 Downing Street. At the 2008 Democratic Convention she wore a green dress that was just too tight and, well, not exactly the best look for her. That "wow" you heard from the women in the press box, liberals and conservatives alike, was not a good thing. But when I pointed this out, Mrs. Obama's defenders tore me up on the Internet. "She likes to dress for her man," one Obama supporter and friend said to me. "We can take it or leave it. That's who she is."

So it appears we are entering the "Age of Michelle." It is one in which she is going to set her own trends and make her own fashion statements, and the rest of us can go sit in a puddle if we don't like it. We never could have gotten away with that in Washington in the early 1990s, so maybe it's a harbinger of change and not all bad. On the other hand, I still don't think you could get away with it in New York—eventually you'd have to give in. In Washington it's a courageous act, even if we don't have our own "Fashion Week" down here! Maybe Mrs. Obama thinks she doesn't need anyone to mentor her in this regard.

But I know that I would not have gotten as far as I have without my own mentors who steered me toward good hairdressers competent to handle my needs and away from those old St. John knits!

I was personally disappointed, during the 2008 election, that so few women chose to reach out a nurturing hand to Sarah Palin. So few realized how vital it is to nurture another woman as she is seeking the powerful position all women have so far in the history of this country been denied. I was shocked, frankly, that, beyond the lack of support for Palin's candidacy, much of the vitriol came from other women. I've written this book in hopes that we can raise the level of discourse and learn the lesson of supporting each other when the next woman takes her turn for the presidency. There isn't one woman we are all going to like. But what's important is that we stand together to make sure that the discussion remains grounded in issues of substance, not what we don't like about her as a woman.

8

WHAT DO WOMEN
DO N.O.W.?

THE NEED TO NATIONALLY
ORGANIZE WOMEN

*T*HE 2008 ELECTION, and the lessons it teaches, shows women the way to keep moving forward. The best way for us to triumph over the sexism that is endemic to the political system is for us to organize—not as liberals or conservatives, but as proud women—and with the men who care as much about this as we do.

Chapter 1 of this book included a discussion of the "mean girls" phenomenon, how we can be a little bit chatty and a whole lot of catty about each other once someone steps out into the public eye. Whether it's Hillary Clinton or Sarah Palin, Michelle Obama or Cindy McCain, we can all find things about them we don't like and we can all spend hours—and some of us did spend hours—dissecting the ways in which they come up short.

Rosalind Wiseman's book *Queen Bees and Wannabes: Helping Your Daughter Survive Cliques, Gossip, Boyfriends, and Other Realities of Adolescence,* as I explained earlier, was the basis for the

2004 motion picture *Mean Girls,* a movie whose plot, I suspect, is all too familiar to many of us.

In an April 2009 interview with me, Wiseman explained, "Women love to talk to me about the legacy that we bring from girls to women, and how we respond to each other, especially in moments of competition and conflict.

"That's what politics is," she told me.

Men and women, and this should come as a surprise to no one, view, experience, and react differently to politics, something I think this book worked to articulate in a succinct and meaningful way. Until now, women had to seek office within the confines of a system that did not, on the surface, at least, develop in ways that are consistent with our natural strengths—and which did not necessarily see a role for women in it. But the system is changing, as are the ways in which people will be elected to office and the tools on which they will rely to do so.

In the future, as the number of independent voters continues to rise and party affiliation continues to soften, superior organizational and socially inclusive skills will become paramount. The advances in technology, the advent of social media, and the acceleration they facilitate have proven that they are real political tools that have created openings for women to redefine, in an appreciable manner, the way in which campaigns are conducted across the country.

But this may also require us to change the way we conduct business ourselves.

"As a generational value," Wiseman says, "many women who are in positions of leadership are in the second tier of feminism. It's not just a stereotype that they are micromanaging. It's an experience that many, many people have."

What Wiseman is describing is not too far removed from Hollywood's idea of the pushy broad, the stage mother, the know-it-all who cozies up to male managers in order to secure her position in the workplace by becoming the office snitch. None of us wants to be that person but, as I have seen in a number of campaigns in which I have participated, somebody almost always is.

Part of this comes from an impulse that produces, as Wiseman says, "this feeling that if I don't do it, it's not going to get done.

"It's Mom who bitches and moans about everyone not cleaning up after themselves," she says, because it means she has to clean up after everybody else. "It's a real failure because it also means that I do think there is a degree of serious truth—to a subsequent generation who do not feel mentored by that group of women." By listening, and letting ourselves be mentored, we may find ourselves able to make our mark on our own terms, under our own rules.

So the first step toward this is to embrace some attributes of these older generations of feminist women (rather than push them away, as we saw younger voters do to Hillary Clinton) and learn from their experiences. As Wiseman advises, we need to let them serve as our teachers and to build on the lessons they provide, whether we are Republicans or Democrats.

"I have made a point in my life to seek out women who are in their sixties who are my mentors," Wiseman says. "But you really have to seek it out."

Listening will occasionally require us younger women to hold our tongues. "I don't think we're going to get past some of the issues," Wiseman says, "until we engage in a dialogue where older women are able to sit at the table and say 'Okay, I acknowledge that that is your experience.' I'm not going to listen to that and immediately react and say, 'No, that's not my experience.'"

"You are being disrespectful to your elders," Wiseman says of the women who gave Hillary Clinton and Sarah Palin the brush off. "In Latin, 'respect' literally means to look back on somebody's achievements. If you have an experience with somebody where they are constantly not giving you the capacity, confidence, or ways in which to engage in meaningful ways, or are micromanaging all the time, then you are not going to respect them."

Together, we have to decide who we are and who we want to be. And we need to understand how we function as what some have called a "movement" but is really a diverse collection of interests and expertise coming together under the umbrella of being women.

In her 1974 paper "Political Organization in the Feminist Movement," Jo Freeman wrote, "A social movement is a very complex and little understood phenomenon. It involves various mixtures of spontaneous and structured ingredients aimed at some combination of personal and/or institutional change. Thus it is often difficult to tease out the salient factors which determine its character and the nature of its activities." Freeman went on to detail the fact that social movements have both informal structures and formal organizations.[1]

We've come a long way since 1974. To this point, what the 2008 election showed us is that women may be ready to abandon the identity-making cohesion we once felt to formal organizations on the left and right in favor of informal structures, like groups that come together on the Internet. These groups don't really have leaders—they are more like high-tech coffee klatches that can accomplish a great deal.

Establishing the mentor-mentee relationship between different generations of politically active women is the first step down the road toward breaking out of the box others have put us in since we won the right to vote. And once we are talking *to* each other, rather than *at* each other, we can focus on developing organizations that allow us to compete as equals in the political arena. And the best place to start this process is online.

Andrew Rasiej, the founder of Personal Democracy Forum, an annual conference and Web site that covers the intersection of politics and technology, told me, "Politics often is framed by people talking to each other." Rasiej, who presided over a group blog, TechPresident.com, which covered how the 2008 presidential candidates used the Web, emphasized that the major difference election to election is that "the speed is exponentially greater than four years ago."[2]

The ability to move quickly in cyberspace, to broadcast messages, to flag and draw attention to issues that might otherwise have gone unnoticed, and to virtually collaborate with extremely low transition costs, is a big part of leveling the political playing field going forward, in terms of resources and their allocation, as well as campaign structure.

In our interview, Rasiej cited as an example the flap that occurred after Obama's perceived July 2008 flip-flop on the issue of warrantless wiretaps, a particularly important issue to the anti-war and anti-Bush activist blocs that were helping him win the nomination.

In fact, according to NPR, "one of the most vocal criticisms of Obama's reversal on the issue comes from a group on the candidate's own social networking site, My.barackobama.com. The group's Web page exhorts, 'Senator Obama—Please Vote NO on Telecom Immunity—Get FISA Right.'[3]"

In all, over twenty thousand Obama supporters protested the vote—putting Obama's campaign on unsure footing. Until, that is, Obama responded directly to their concerns using all the communications tools available, especially those afforded by the Web.

"He said, 'I hear you. I don't agree. There are so many other things we agree upon that we shouldn't let this stop us from reaching our goal.' And then he made his policy people available for the next three hours," Rasiej said, explaining how Obama and his campaign effectively extinguished the fire.

Salon contributing writer Glenn Greenwald gave "genuine credit to him for being responsive this way and for having his site be a forum for disagreement among his supporters and himself. Providing a forum for those sorts of debates is a sign of a secure and healthy campaign."[4] Not only was this an effective communications strategy, but it also created a new set of expectations of and for the modern-day politician. In effect, his constituents asked for and received Obama's feedback through the direct and more egalitarian model of political engagement.

The critical question facing women who want to expand our political and cultural influence is how we build effective followings for individuals and causes using constantly changing and evolving technologies. And, further, how we will do this with the direct and two-way communications paradigm in mind?

By the next election faxing will be nearly dead and e-mailing will have evolved at least another generation with regard to the science of production, metrics, management, and efficacy—social media changed all that. Specifically, technological innovations, social media adoption, and our desire to do more, know more, and affect more are the driving factors behind these dramatic shifts. In this new rubric, candidates and campaigns will be encouraged—or forced—to develop ways to manage an enormous, ever-changing information stream. Nuggets of actionable information and intelligence will be sifted from this fire hose of raw data, using various filters that allow people to discover things of interest to them, often while they might be searching for something else. Social responses to social information will be immediate, and its impact will be almost instantaneous.

This 24/7 informational serendipity will have a far-reaching impact, nurturing a far more volatile political landscape where the hot topic of the moment can change, literally with the viral currency of a single bit of text in a message appearing before only one small group, but with a very large following. A 140-character "tweet" can potentially carry the political and social power that once required thousands of printing presses, or massive banks of phones, fax machines, or web server farms.

This viral propensity encourages discovery—and that means swarms of attention and action can form in minutes, with almost no organizational infrastructure and no money. Imagine a set of bees swarming around a comb of honey. They need only the scent of the nutrient to trigger the swarm.

Compare this to the past, when the key people making an impact on the political landscape needed resources, connections, labor, and time. Women have always been good organizers but they never had infrastructure. Tomorrow's political leaders will be those who master social media, which economizes all of those things. If you tell a credible story and articulate it well, followers, thanks to the convergence of this technology, will find you—

quickly. Hence, the political capital of the future will be friends, credibility, and followers. In fact, the social Web already has a name for it—"whuffie." The concept, first introduced by Cory Doctorow in 2003, has since been turned into a moniker du jour for social media communities. Author and marketing consultant Tara Hunt released an entire book dedicated to the subject in April 2009 called *The Whuffie Factor.*

What Freeman wrote about the women's movement in its early days—"This laissez-faire philosophy of organizing has allowed the talents of many women to develop spontaneously and others to learn skills they didn't know"—is going to be true as we move forward. And it will also be true, however we find ourselves coming together, that we will have to find ways to deal with the problem, as Freeman observed, "that most groups are unwilling to change their structure when they change their tasks. They have accepted the ideology of 'structurelessness' without realizing the limitations of its uses. . . . This means that the movement is essentially run, locally, by women who can work at it full time."

One who does is Teri Christoph, a Virginia homemaker who is one of the leaders of an organization called Smart Girl Politics, which was formed online in response to the 2008 election and has been active against the Obama stimulus and in fomenting the "tea party" demonstrations.

Christoph cites as her major concerns the passing of federal debt onto her children and the limits it places on her own family's pocketbooks. By existing online, the Smart Girls can encourage debate and dialogue among a wide audience that will help empower conservative women. "We tried to create a place where anyone who self-identifies as a conservative, but they do not have to check a list." They wanted to create a space where women are "respectful" of one another, she told me.[5] By being online, they also created their own virtual and permanent footprint that could be found, traced, and extended by others.

"Though there is such a difference between Sarah Palin and Hillary Clinton, they were both treated equally badly," Christoph said. "They said Palin wasn't a leading intellectual, and she got attacked for it. Hillary Clinton is an intellectual, and she got attacked for that. What would the perfect candidate look like—one that wouldn't get attacked? She doesn't exist."

Christoph and the Smart Girls are part of a new breed of younger women who are using the Web to find their political voice, unencumbered by the need to carve out a spot from what already exists in a limited space.

Another is Meghan McCain, on whom the national spotlight first fell during her father's 2008 run for president. Her blog, McCainBlogette.com, provided an inside look at the campaign as seen through the eyes of a younger voter.

Part of the challenge we face is the development of ground rules or "best practices" that will help us, as women, maximize our success and our potential for success. Liza Sabater, the founder and lead blogger at CultureKitchen.com, a popular community blog for activists, told me in an interview this is "absolutely necessary."[6]

"I do believe it's absolutely necessary to change the whole dynamic of how we teach women to defend themselves," Sabater told me. "Part of the issue, socially speaking, is [that] even in the professional world, women tend to be relegated to the private aspect of life. So even if a major company has small gender disparities amongst its vice presidents, the public face of the company is usually male."

This is an idea that applies particularly to the younger McCain, who has built a following urging the GOP to rebrand itself by reversing course on social issues like same-sex marriage. Her efforts remind us of the importance of the need to appeal across generations—especially to the Millennials, who came of age after the collapse of the Berlin Wall.

The polling data indicates that these voters are more interested in fiscal responsibility and less government involvement in private behavior, particularly where sexual matters are concerned, and are greener and more civic minded than the generation that immediately preceded them. These are all important issues and, for the most part, are ones that involve more than a slight element of emotion—which makes Sabater's call for ground rules and best practices all the more important.

Just as it is in the political world, there are too few women in the business world who would be considered "captains of industry." Part of that is cultural—and it is changing fast. Just look at Meg Whitman and Carla Fiorina, who came out of the business world to hold prominent positions in the McCain campaign. But as fast as it's changing, it's still too slow.

In politics, the stereotypes ascribed to women continue to dominate the way they are covered and, as a consequence, whether or not they can conduct effective campaigns. "On the political side, in terms of government, usually women who are very much in the public eye—Palin, Clinton, Pelosi—are called 'bitches,' 'ballbusters,' or 'maneaters,'" Sabater told me, with more than a hint of irritation. "But you would never call Nydia Velásquez [a New York House Democrat] or Olympia Snowe [a Maine Senate Republican] that. They're more on the private end of the government sphere. Even though some people may know who they are, they are not the actual faces of government."

Sabater, like Rasiej, points to the opportunities the Internet holds for women to increase their ability to lay claim to their stake in the political world. "If there is anything that should be done," she says, "it is to really look at digital literacy and image. We're still debating reading, writing, and arithmetic, but the United States is still one of the most media-illiterate countries in terms of how people use the Internet and how they interact in it. Social etiquette is created online.

"A lot of the girls who use Facebook and MySpace behave as though their sites were really private spaces. A lot of women come to me and say, 'I hate those sites online. I'm being smeared. I want to close my comments section because I'm threatened.' My advice has always been, 'You are better than that. You are the one in control.'

"Part of the problem," Sabater continued, "is that we still have older generations in power who are using old, outdated protocols and etiquette concerning acceptable and unacceptable behavior.

While the new social mores are being developed, we need to teach our kids how to deal with the media, how to use it and strategize their own identity online."

In *Mean Girls,* the pathway to success came from standing resolute in the face of attacks. Today's successful women in the political and business worlds alike have learned to respond by establishing the skill sets, expertise, and credentials to overcome long-standing obstacles. This is how respect is earned.

"We need more women to put their foot down. They need to not be afraid because a lot of smearing happens online. Bullies know their victims feel threatened," Sabater said, explaining that that is the reason they do it in the first place.

The answer, says Sabater, is to teach girls to say, "Your words are not threatening to me." This, of course, represents a sea change in the way women have been taught in the last fifteen years or so to deal with problems. In a culture rife with political correctness, we are teaching women to say exactly the opposite. We are teaching them to let their tormentors know that their words, and merely their words, are threatening, and to use that charge like a weapon against people with whom we disagree.

In my judgment, that's not the way forward. As women, if we want to truly be successful, to really be equal, we have to learn to fend for ourselves. We can't expect somebody else, whether it's Daddy or our big brothers or college administrators or human resources people to fight our battles for us every time we get our feelings hurt. We need to teach ourselves, and each other, to stand up and say, "No—that's not right—and I deserve better."

Deborah Price, the former assistant deputy secretary in the Office of Safe and Drug Free Schools at the U.S. Department of Education, agrees that this is a subtle skill.

"I think we are raising a generation of kids who are walking around with a big chip on their shoulder," she told me in a June 2009 interview, "demanding respect and retaliating when they don't get it. What these kids don't comprehend is that respect isn't something you can demand or require; it is something you earn or give."

But, as I said, it's all about how you ask for it. "The problem with people demanding respect is they get angry when they don't get it," Price said. "I see a lot of this, especially in young girls. And the down side of this is girl-on-girl violence, anything from the typical mean-girl bullying to actual physical violence." It should also be noted that social media, in some ways, has helped to underscore and amplify this phenomenon. YouTube served as the conduit through which instances of adolescent girl-on-girl violence were documented and spread.[7]

Which may be one of the lessons we can take away from Hillary Clinton's complaints about the way she was treated by *Saturday Night Live.* Yes, they were pro-Obama. Yes, she was getting the short end of the stick. But it's a comedy show, not *Meet the Press.* And picking that fight, and the way she asked for better treatment, came across as special pleading and whining—and that's the way it was reported. Not to put it all on her shoulders, because she did have a legitimate point—and so did Sarah Palin, but you didn't hear her complaining about Tina Fey; in fact, you saw her standing next to her for a brief second before Tina rushed off the stage—but Hillary Clinton needed to think long and hard about how she asked for respect before she opened her mouth.

As Sabater puts it, "We really need more Amazons online. We need to have more women who will say 'You can't get away with this' and who won't show fear. That's the most important thing—and that's why knowing the technology is more important. There are ways to block people. If you don't understand tech and how to use it strategically in these cases, we're always going to be crying foul or thinking of ourselves as the victim."

But that doesn't mean we have to become better or smarter bullies. It means we have to think smart and remember, as Sun Tzu might of said, the best victories come in the battles we never have to fight.

"Rarely are kids today taught conflict resolution," Price said, "so their only way to resolve conflict is through violence."

She argues that today's young people, really everyone today, show little tolerance for opinions that differ from the ones they hold. This was especially clear in the case of Sarah Palin, who saw her femininity and her womanhood questioned repeatedly because other women disagreed with her positions on abortion, guns, taxes, and national defense.

"Sure, a lot of people talk tolerance, and they are pretty good at it until someone disagrees with their opinion," says Price.

And that means, like it or not, we have to take ownership of our behavior. And we can't keep casting about for someone else to blame. That doesn't mean we have to walk around, stoop shouldered, admitting everything is our fault each time someone says something stupid. It means, as Price says, that we have to embrace a definition of responsibility that includes the "ability to respond."

One person who knows this firsthand is Tami Nantz, who created the blog Moms4SarahPalin.net, which I mentioned earlier. In October 2008 Nantz was interviewed on CNN regarding her blog and support for Palin.

"The night the piece aired, the attacks on me and my family started," she said. They were forced to change their phone number and, ultimately, to move. And even with that Nantz says, the harassment continued with late-night prank calls that never seemed to end.

"I wasn't surprised that some people didn't care for what I had to say," Nantz adds. "But I was shocked by the extent of the hate. I have a section on my blog about halfway down on the sidebar called 'The Bellevue Section' in which there are some comments. The ones toward the bottom are the worst, and there are links to many more at the bottom as well. Also, I, along with my husband and two friends, spent hours deleting thousands of comments that had been left that were just vile. They were all left the night the CNN piece aired. I hadn't set my comments to be moderated because I had only had about 10,000 hits up to that point."

Nevertheless, her experience has given her the desire to keep going, to be a new voice in the political world, despite how discouraging it was at times. "Every time I have thoughts of throwing in the towel, I will have someone email me, leave a comment on Facebook or Twitter or come up to me when I'm out and tell me how inspired they have been because of my blog.

"I have had young girls who just voted for the first time in their lives tell me how deeply they appreciate the work I put into the blog and how much they've gotten out of it. People (primarily women) who have never been the least bit interested in politics before this election have thanked me and continue to visit the blog often," Nantz said.

$\mathcal{I}$T MIGHT SEEM as if organizations such as Moms4SarahPalin.net had the wind taken out of their sails on July 3, 2009, when Palin resigned from the governorship of Alaska. But Sarah Palin is a young woman—so young that she can afford to wait out the next six presidential elections and, in 2032, be only as old as McCain was when he sought the White House in 2008.

Nevertheless, whether Palin can ever mount a successful bid for the GOP nomination depends on several key factors. One, can she persuade her base to stick with her now that she has chosen to campaign outside the system instead of (as Hillary Clinton did) from within? Two, will she use her time out of office to develop one or two signature issues that will burnish her intellectual and political credentials—like Reagan on tax cuts or Clinton on health care? Three, can she establish—or re-establish—a relationship with suburban and college-educated women, whose help she will need? Can she bridge the "small-town conservative values" she articulates so well and the intellectual and political heft these women demand? And, finally, can she learn the discipline that is necessary for projecting an image as a confident, competent politician, which has been so sorely lacking in her public communications, at least during the time from the end of the vice presidential campaign to the announcement of her leaving the governorship?

She seems willing to try—and her July 2009 op-ed for the *Washington Post* on cap-and-trade legislation may have been the beginning of that effort. Of course, rather than deal with the substance of what she said, the political chattering class dismissed it as the product of a ghostwriter.

*I*LL CLOSE WITH ONE last tidbit of hope for the future: the effect that the 2008 election had on our young people, especially girls. To gauge the impact of the 2008 presidential election on young Americans, the Girl Scout Research Institute (GSRI) conducted a survey of thirteen- to-seventeen-year-old girls and boys immediately after the election. The study recorded positive effects from the 2008 election—both in terms of gender and race—on young people's confidence, in their own ability to bring about change, and in their attitudes toward leadership.

According to the GSRI, "59 percent of girls and 52 percent of boys reported that the election had a positive impact on their confidence in being able to achieve their goals in the future, and 51 percent of girls and 45 percent of boys said it positively impacted their confidence in being able to change things in this country."[9]

Perhaps most interesting for the subject of this book, substantial numbers of young people (46 percent of girls and 38 percent of boys) reported "that they think more highly of women's ability to lead than they did before the election." And, at the same time, the election also helped them to understand "the difficulties women face in reaching leadership positions in our country," with 43 percent of girls believing that "girls have to work harder than boys in order to gain positions of leadership," which was up from 25 percent in a similar survey in 2007.

Overall, "a large majority of girls (82 percent) and boys (72 percent) agreed that 'girls and boys are equally good at being leaders,' although girls are more likely than boys to strongly agree with the statement"; 75 percent of girls said that "they were excited about the two female candidates." And "71 percent of girls believe it is likely that a woman will be elected as president in the United States within the next ten years. Twenty-two percent believe it will 'definitely' happen."[10]

I sure hope they're right. I think we can all agree that: it is to our advantage as a nation and to our benefit as a society to have more—not fewer—people engaged in the political sphere. Whether they are candidates for office, government employees, staffers, activists, or just engaged voters, the point is: the bigger the pie, the better. And it's my belief that this will benefit us all—men and women, Republicans and Democrats, people of all races, ethnicities, religions, and backgrounds.

But to make this a reality—especially when it comes to women in politics—we must make some conscious changes in how we operate. And, I'll be honest, this wasn't necessarily a conclusion I thought I'd reach in writing this book. But, throughout the course of writing, it became clear to me that the way we treat each other in the course of political campaigns and discourse—particularly, how we treat women in the public eye—is detrimental. It's holding us back as women and as a nation. Let me be clear: I'm not arguing for a special set of rules for women or kid-glove treatment for female candidates. Far from it.

Instead, I'm challenging us all—myself included—to raise our level of awareness and then act accordingly. We need to think about how what we say and do to women political candidates affects not just the current election cycle, but also how it affects the many young adults—and girls and boys out there—who are paying attention. And we need to *care* about what it means.

Right now, there is virtually no penalty for unfairly tearing down women. No penalty for members of the media, and virtually none from the voters (men and women). Talking at length about Hillary Clinton's pantsuits or analyzing how many pounds she may have gained on the campaign trail is not viewed as anything out of the ordinary. Endless cable chatter devoted to Sarah Palin's makeup, glasses, and wardrobe is just part of our political lexicon. (And that's to say nothing of how her family was treated.) It's par for the course, right? Well no, actually.

That's the point. We accept it almost by accident. I know I did. But it's about knowing how what we say in the media—and what we accept as consumers of that media—influences our own attitudes, voting preferences, and our children's perceptions of the political world.

*I*T'S TRUE WE'VE come a long way, but we have even farther to go, and how we get there—how we treat each other in the process—may just determine how quickly we achieve true parity for women in U.S. politics, or if we ever do.

NOTES

INTRODUCTION: YOU'VE COME A LONG WAY, MAYBE

1. The Las Comadres website can be found at http://www.genders .org/g28/g28_lascomadres.html.
2. Domenico Montanaro, "McCain Camp Palin Fundraising," MSNBC, September 1, 2008, http://firstread.msnbc.msn.com/archive/2008/09/01/1320 772.aspx. Accessed July 23, 2009.
3. Robin Givhan, "Hillary Clinton's Tentative Dip into New Neckline Territory," *Washington Post,* July 20, 2007, http://www.washingtonpost.com/ wp-dyn/content/article/2007/07/19/AR2007071902668.html. Accessed July 23, 2009.
4. Chris Matthews on *Morning Joe,* MSNBC, January 9, 2008.
5. AskMen.com, "Blog of the Day: Is Sarah Palin Hot?" September 3, 2008, http://www.askmen.com/daily/blogs/women/is-sarah-palin-hot.html. Accessed July 23, 2009.
6. Charlotte Allen, "We Scream, We Swoon. How Dumb Can We Get?" *Washington Post,* March 2, 2008, http://www.washingtonpost.com/ wp-dyn/content/article/2008/02/29/AR2008022902992.html.
7. Interview with Rosalind Wiseman, author of *Queen Bees and Wannabes: Helping Your Daughter Survive Cliques, Gossip, Boyfriends, and Other Realities of Adolescence,* April 22, 2009.
8. Lifetime Networks, "Every Woman Counts," December 3, 2008.
9. Campbell Brown, "Cutting Through the Bull," CNN, October 22, 2008.
10. Katie Couric, *CBS Evening News,* June 11, 2008, http://www.cbsnews.com/ blogs/2008/06/11/couricandco/entry4174429.shtml. Accessed July 23, 2009.
11. Jezebel.com, October 28, 2008, http://jezebel.com/5069986/as-far-as-im-concerned-former-ms-editor-elaine-lafferty-can-go-f+ck-herself. Accessed July 23, 2009.
12. Frank Newport, "Michelle Obama's Speech Could Make a Difference," Gallup, August 25, 2008.
13. Gallup, "Favorability: People in the News," from survey period September 5–7, 2008, http://www.gallup.com/poll/1618/favorability-people-news.aspx. Accessed July 23, 2009.

14. Patrick Healy, "New to Campaigning, but No Longer a Novice," *New York Times,* October 27, 2008.
15. Remarks by Michelle Obama, Milwaukee, Wisconsin, February 18, 2008 [widely reported].
16. Anne E. Kornblut, "Michelle Obama's Career Timeout," *Washington Post,* May 11, 2007, http://www.washingtonpost.com/wp-dyn/content/article/2007/05/10/AR2007051002573.html. Accessed July 11, 2009.
17. Interview with Candy Crowley, CNN senior political correspondent, March 3, 2009.
18. Women's Voices. Women Vote, press release, "Single Women Prove Decisive Political Force," November 5, 2008, http://www.wvwv.org/2008/11/5/single-women-prove-decisive-political-force.
19. Camille Paglia, "Fresh Blood for the Vampire," Salon.com, September 10, 2008, http://www.salon.com/opinion/paglia/2008/09/10/palin/index.html. Accessed July 23, 2009.
20. All polls reported by Polling Report at http://www.pollingreport.com/politics.htm.
21. Lifetime Networks, "Every Woman Counts," December 3, 2008.
22. Girl Scout Research Institute, "The New Leadership Landscape: What Girls Say about Election 2008," January 13, 2009, http://www.girlscouts.org/news/news_releases/2009/leadership_landscape_2008_summary.pdf. Accessed July 23, 2009.
23. Frank Newport, "Americans See Obama Election as Race Relations Milestone," Gallup, November 7, 2008, http://www.gallup.com/poll/111817/americans-see-obama-election-race-relations-milestone.aspx. Accessed July 23, 2009.
24. Girl Scout Research Institute, "The New Leadership Landscape: What Girls Say about Election 2008," January 13, 2009, http://www.girlscouts.org/news/news_releases/2009/leadership_landscape_2008_summary.pdf. Accessed July 23, 2009.

CHAPTER 1: THE SISTERHOOD OF THE TRAVELING PANTSUITS

1. Interview with Hilary Rosen, editor-at-large for the Huffington Post and CNN political contributor, March 28, 2009.
2. Anne E. Kornblut and Matthew Mosk, "Clinton Owes Lead in Poll to Support from Women," *Washington Post,* June 12, 2007, A01.
3. Interview with Candy Crowley, CNN senior political correspondent, March 3, 2009.
4. Anne E. Kornblut and Matthew Mosk, "Clinton Owes Lead in Poll To Support From Women," *Washington Post,* June 12, 2007, A01.
5. Lydia Saad, "Clinton Retains Strong Lead in Democratic Field," Gallup, September 13, 2007.
6. Interview with Hilary Rosen, editor-at-large for the Huffington Post and CNN political contributor, March 28, 2009.
7. David Paul Kuhn, "Iowa voters reveal unexpected trends," Politico.com, January 4, 2008.

8. Dan Gerstein, "The Republican Renaissance Gap," Forbes.com, April, 1, 2009, http://www.forbes.com/2009/03/31/republican-relevance-gap-opin ions-columnists-gop.html. Accessed July 23, 2009.

9. "Candidates Strive to Address Voter Concerns on Economy," January 10, 2008. http://www.pbs.org/newshour/bb/business/jan-june08/economy_01– 10.html. Accessed July 11, 2009.

10. Interview with Rachel Sklar, former political editor at the Huffington Post and a subsequent contributor to The Daily Beast, February 27, 2009.

11. Ibid.

12. Interview with Patti Solis Doyle, former campaign manager for Hillary Clinton's 2008 presidential campaign, April 2, 2009.

13. Interview with Candy Crowley, CNN senior political correspondent, March 3, 2009.

14. Joshua Green, "The Front-Runner's Fall," *The Atlantic,* September 2008.

15. Dan Morain, "Iowa Can't Be Bought, History Shows," *Los Angeles Times,* January 3, 2008.

16. Jeffrey M. Jones, "Obama, Clinton Tied in New Hampshire," Gallup, December 31, 2007.

17. Democratic Primary Debate, Manchester, New Hampshire, January 5, 2008, as broadcast on ABC News.

18. Richard Cohen, "'You're Likable Enough' Costs Obama," Real Clear Politics, January 10, 2008, www.realclearpolitics.com.

19. MSNBC, "Countdown with Keith Olbermann," April 23, 2008. http:// www.msnbc.msn.com/id/24293391/. Accessed July 11, 2009.

20. Rachel Sklar, "Keith Olbermann's Idea For Beating Hillary: Literally Beating Hillary," HuffingtonPost.com, April 25, 2008, http://www.huffington post.com/2008/04/25/keith-olbermanns-idea-for_n_98557.html.

21. Lester Holt, MSNBC, February 5, 2008, as reported by "Media Matters for America," February 6, 2008.

22. SkyNews, "Hillary Clinton's Bid for White House Hit by 'Sexist' Protest," January 8, 2008, http://news.sky.com/skynews/Home/Sky-News-Archive/ Article/20080641299766. Accessed July 11, 2009.

23. Interview with Candy Crowley, CNN senior political correspondent, March 3, 2009.

24. "To my supporters, my champions—my sisterhood of the traveling pantsuits—from the bottom of my heart: Thank you." Hillary Clinton, Democratic National Convention, Denver, Colorado, August 26, 2008.

25. Margaret Doris, "The Sisterhood of the Traveling Pantsuit, Divided," *Esquire,* August 29, 2008.

26. Dan Balz and Jon Cohen, "Democrats Willing to Let Battle Continue," *Washington Post,* April 16, 2008, A1.

27. Adam Nagourney and Jeff Zeleny, "Clinton Uses Sharp Attacks in Tense Debate," *New York Times,* April 17, 2008.

28. Hillary Clinton, Speech to Supporters, Washington, D.C., June 7, 2008.

29. Hillary Clinton, Democratic National Convention, Denver, Colorado, August 26, 2008.

30. *Saturday Night Live,* May 10, 2008.

31. Dick Morris and Eileen McGann, "Hillary's Campaign Against Obama Continues," Newsmax.com, August 14, 2008.
32. Katie Couric, *CBS Evening News,* June 11, 2008, http://www.cbsnews.com/blogs/2008/06/11/couricandco/entry4174429.shtml. Accessed July 23, 2009.
33. Interview with Candy Crowley, CNN senior political correspondent, March 3, 2009.
34. Lois Romano, "Clinton Puts Up a New Fight," *Washington Post,* May 20, 2008, C1.

CHAPTER 2: THE PALIN EFFECT

1. John Solomon, "Splitting Hairs, Edwards's Stylist Tells His Side of Story," *Washington Post,* July 5, 2007.
2. MSNBC Potomac Primary Coverage, February 13, 2008.
3. William E. Gibson, "Finding The Perfect Fit," *Sun-Sentinel* (Fort Lauderdale, Florida), July 20, 2008.
4. Jack Kelly, "McCain's Secret Weapon," *Pittsburgh Post-Gazette,* June 8, 2008.
5. Nate Silver, "The Palin Paradox: Women More Likely to be Elected in Male-Dominated Districts," June 7, 2009, http://www.fivethirtyeight.com/2009/06/palin-paradox-women-more-likely-to-be.html. Accessed July 11, 2009.
6. The Rush Limbaugh Show, "Sarah Palin: Babies, Guns, Jesus," August 29, 2008, http://www.rushlimbaugh.com/home/daily/site_082908/content/0112 5111.guest.html. Accessed July 11, 2009.
7. Gallup Daily Tracking Poll, 2008 Presidential Election, http://www.gallup.com/poll/107674/Gallup-Daily-Election-2008.aspx. Accessed July 23, 2009.
8. Lifetime Networks, "New Lifetime Every Woman Counts Poll Reveals McCain/Palin and Obama/Biden in Tight Race for the Women's Vote, with This Critical Voting Bloc Split on Key Presidential Attributes," September 22, 2008, PRnewswire.com.
9. John Cohen and Dan Balz, "In Poll, McCain Closes the Gap with Obama," *Washington Post,* September 9, 2008.
10. Nielsen Wire, "Palin Triggers RNC Ratings Spike," September 4, 2008, http://blog.nielsen.com/nielsenwire/media_entertainment/palin-triggers-rnc-ratings-spike/. Accessed July 23, 2009.
11. Alaska governor Sarah Palin, Republican National Convention, September 3, 2008.
12. *U.S. News & World Report,* Political Bulletin, September 4, 2008.
13. Camille Paglia, "Fresh Blood for the Vampire," Salon.com, September 10, 2008.
14. Ron Nessen, "Sarah Palin: A Good Surprise," Brookings Institution, August 31, 2008.
15. Brian Ross, "$10 Million Woman: Palin a Hit with GOP Donors," ABC News, September 1, 2008.
16. William March, "Florida Fans Break Sweat At Palin Rally," *Tampa Tribune,* September 22, 2008.

17. Mason Admans, "Thousands Turn out for Palin," *Roanoke Times,* October 28, 2008.
18. Interview with John C. Abell, New York Bureau Chief of Wired.com, April 1, 2009.
19. Available at http://urbanlegends.about.com/library/bl_anne_kilkenny_on _palin.htm. Accessed July 23, 2009.
20. Available at http://www.factcheck.org/elections–2008/sliming_palin.html. Accessed June 11, 2009. Accessed July 23, 2009.
21. Interview by e-mail with Liz Mair, former RNC online communications director, April 4, 2009.
22. Ibid.
23. "Tweet" is a term used to describe a post on a real-time social networking and micro-blogging Web site called Twitter.
24. Gallup Daily Tracking Poll, 2008 Presidential Election, http://www.gallup .com/poll/107674/Gallup-Daily-Election–2008.aspx. Accessed July 23, 2009.
25. Liz Halloran, "McCain Suspends Campaign, Shocks Republicans," *U.S. News & World Report,* September 24, 2008.
26. Pew Research Center's Project for Excellence in Journalism, "VEEP Debate, Palin Rule Campaign News," September 29–October 5, 2008.
27. *Saturday Night Live,* October 4, 2008.
28. Monica Langley, "Game Plan for Palin Is Retooled Ahead of Debate: Top McCain Aides Oversee Preparation After Recent Flubs," *Wall Street Journal,* September 29, 2008.
29. Ibid.
30. Pew Research Center's Project for Excellence in Journalism, "VEEP Debate, Palin Rule Campaign News," September 29–October 5, 2008.
31. Andrew Kohut and Kim Parker, "SNL Appearance, Wardrobe Flap Register Widely: PALIN FATIGUE NOW RIVALS OBAMA FATIGUE," The Pew Research Center for the People and the Press, October 29, 2008.
32. Rasmussen Reports, "Palin Power: Fresh Face Now More Popular Than Obama, McCain," September 5, 2008.
33. Gallup, "Favorability: People in the News," http://www.gallup.com/poll/ 1618/Favorability-People-News.aspx#1. Accessed July 23, 2009.
34. Pew Research Center's Project for Excellence in Journalism, "VEEP Debate, Palin Rule Campaign News," September 29–October 5, 2008.
35. Ross Douthat, "Palin-Biden!!!!," *The Atlantic,* October 3, 2008.
36. Kate Zernike, "She Just Might Be President Someday," *New York Times,* May 18, 2008.
37. CNN, "Newsroom," August 29, 2008.
38. Jodi Kantor and Rachel L. Swarns, "A New Twist in the Debate on Mothers," *New York Times,* September 1, 2008.
39. John F. Harris and Beth Frerking, "Clinton Aides: Palin Treatment Sexist," Politico.com, September 3, 2008.
40. Robin Abcarian, "Sarah Palin's 'New Feminism' Is Hailed," *Los Angeles Times,* September 4, 2008.
41. Robin Givhan, "Sarah Palin's Unassertive Fashion Statement," *Washington Post,* September 28, 2008.

42. Rich Noyes, "ABC Pounds Away at Palin Pregnancy, 'Skeleton in the Closet,'" September 2, 2008, http://newsbusters.org/blogs/rich-noyes/2008/09/02/abc-pounds-away-palin-pregnancy-skeleton-closet. Accessed July 23, 2009.
43. Maureen Dowd, "Vice in Go-Go Boots?," *New York Times,* August 31, 2008.
44. Andrew Kohut and Kim Parker, "SNL Appearance, Wardrobe Flap Register Widely: PALIN FATIGUE NOW RIVALS OBAMA FATIGUE," Pew Research Center for the People and the Press, October 29, 2008.
45. Rich Noyes, "ABC Anchor Impugns Sarah Palin As a Neglectful Mother," August 30, 2008, http://newsbusters.org/blogs/rich-noyes/2008/08/30/abc-anchor-impugns-sarah-palin-neglectful-mother. Accessed July 11, 2009.
46. Debbie Walsh and Susan J. Carroll, "Gender Gap Evident in the 2008 Election: Women, Unlike Men, Show Clear Preference for Obama over McCain," Center for American Women in Politics, Rutgers University, November 5, 2008.
47. Women's Voices. Women Vote, press release, "Single Women Prove Decisive Political Force," November 5, 2008, http://www.wvwv.org/2008/11/5/single-women-prove-decisive-political-force. Accessed July 23, 2009.

CHAPTER 3: WOMEN'S GROUPS AND SARAH PALIN

1. Christian News Wire, "Sarah Palin will make history," August 29, 2008, http://www.christiannewswire.com/news/644377674.html. Accessed June 11, 2009.
2. E-mail interview with Tami Nantz, creator of moms4sarahpalin.net, June 10, 2009.
3. Elaine Lafferty, "Palin's Smart Move," The Daily Beast, March 6, 2009.
4. John F. Harris and Beth Frerking, "Clinton Aides: Palin Treatment Sexist," Politico.com, September 3, 2008.
5. Gloria Steinem, "Palin: Wrong Woman, Wrong Message," *Los Angeles Times,* September 4, 2008, A29.
6. Dee Dee Myers, "Sarah Palin: A Sleight of Gender?" August 29, 2008, http://www.huffingtonpost.com/dee-dee-myers/sarah-palin-the-double-x_b_122447.html. Accessed July 23, 2009.
7. Ibid.
8. Elaine Lafferty, "Sarah Palin's A Brainiac," The Daily Beast, October 27, 2008.
9. Katie Couric, *CBS Evening News,* September 30, 2008.
10. Alaska governor Sarah Palin, Republican National Convention, September 3, 2008.
11. Peter Hamby, "Clinton Backers by Her Side, Palin Makes Pitch to Women Voters," CNN.com, October 21, 2008.
12. Jill Zuckman, "Sarah Palin Responds to Wardrobe Flap," *Chicago Tribune,* October 24, 2008.
13. NPR, "Sarah Palin: New Face of Feminism?," All Things Considered, September 7, 2008.
14. Naomi Schaefer Riley, "Sarah Palin Feminism," *Wall Street Journal,* September 5, 2008.

15. Robin Abcarian, "Sarah Palin's 'New Feminism' Is Hailed," *Los Angeles Times,* September 4, 2008.
16. E-mail interview with April-Liesel Binapri, founder of the Female Alliance of Conservative Equality, April 2, 2009.
17. Feministing.com, September 8, 2008, http://www.feministing.com/archives/010904.html. Accessed July 23, 2009.
18. Jezebel.com, posted October 28, 2008, http://jezebel.com/5069986/as-far-as-im-concerned-former-ms-editor-elaine-lafferty-can-go-f+ck-herself.
19. "Sarah Palin is Not a Feminist," August 30, 2008, http://menstrual poetry.com/sarah-palin-feminist. Accessed July 11, 2009.
20. Olivia St. John, "Sarah Palin's feminist folly," September 2, 2008, http://www.wnd.com/index.php?fa=PAGE.view&pageId=74043. Accessed July 11, 2009.
21. Jin Vandehei and David Paul Kuhn, "Palin Reignites Culture Wars," Politico.com, September 2, 2008, http://www.politico.com/news/stories/0908/13101.html. Accessed July 23, 2009.
22. Tennessee Guerilla Women, "Misogyny Watch: 'Progressive' Menz Count the Months of Sarah Palin's Pregnancies!," August 31, 2008, http://guerilla-womentn.blogspot.com/2008_08_01_archive.html. Accessed July 23, 2009.
23. Liz Hunt, "How Good a 'Mom' Can Sarah Palin Be?," *Daily Telegraph,* http://www.telegraph.co.uk/comment/columnists/lizhunt/3561880/How-good-a-'mom'-can-Sarah-Palin-be.html. Accessed July 23, 2009.
24. Gloria Steinem, "Palin: Wrong Woman, Wrong Message," *Los Angeles Times,* September 4, 2008.
25. Katerine Skiba, "Is Sarah Palin's Star Beginning to Fall?," *U.S. News & World Report,* September 18, 2008.
26. Bonnie Erbe, "Sarah Palin, a Drag Around John McCain's Neck," *U.S. News & World Report,* October 23, 2008, http://www.usnews.com/blogs/erbe/2008/10/23/sarah-palin-a-drag-around-john-mccains-neck.html. Accessed July 12, 2009.
27. Lifetime Networks, "Every Woman Counts," December 3, 2008.
28. Campbell Brown, "Cutting Through the Bull," CNN, October 22, 2008.
29. Cokie Roberts, *Good Morning America,* ABC, August 30, 2008.
30. Tom Baldwin, "Sarah Palin Damned by Faint Praise from America's Leading Women," [London] *Times,* September 9, 2008. Accessed July 23, 2009.
31. Jodi Kantor and Rachel L. Swarns, "A New Twist in the Debate on Mothers," *New York Times,* September 1, 2008.
32. Jim Quinn, "The War Room," Clear Channel Radio, October 6, 2008.
33. Ben Shapiro, "Sexism Rears its Ugly Head," Real Clear Politics, September 3, 2008, http://www.realclearpolitics.com.
34. John F. Harris and Beth Frerking, "Clinton Aides: Palin Treatment Sexist," Politico.com, September 3, 2008.
35. Camille Paglia, "Palin: Feminism's Greatest Leap Forward since Madonna," Salon.com, September 10, 2008, http://www.salon.com/opinion/paglia/2008/09/10/palin/index.html. Accessed July 23, 2009.
36. Christine Todd Whitman, Remarks at the Institute of Politics, John F. Kennedy School of Government, October 29, 1998.

37. Interview with Candy Crowley, CNN senior political correspondent, March 3, 2008.
38. Gloria Steinem, "Palin: Wrong Woman, Wrong Message," *Los Angeles Times,* September 4, 2008.
39. David Kahane, "I Hate You Sarah Palin," *National Review Online,* September 2, 2008, http://article.nationalreview.com/?q=N2YzODI3MGE3 OTU0Yjg5ZDY5YmFjZmE3MmFiOWE4ZjQ=. Accessed July 23, 2009.

CHAPTER 4: WHAT IT TAKES

1. M. Stanton Evan, "The Gender Gap Revisited," *National Review,* September 16, 1988.
2. Isabel Wilkerson, "Milestone for Black Women in Gaining U.S. Senate Seat," *New York Times,* November 4, 1992.
3. Women in Congress, "I'm No Lady; I'm a Member of Congress," http://womenincongress.house.gov/essays/essay1/family-connections.html. Accessed July 19, 2009.
4. Hannelore Suderman, "A Seat at the Table," *Washington State Magazine,* Summer 2009, http://wsm.wsu.edu/s/index.php?id=254. Accessed July 19, 2009.
5. Juliet Eilperin and Matthew Mosk, "McCain Got Palin Fundraising Bounce," *Washington Post,* September 20, 2008.
6. Domenico Montanaro, "McCain Camp Palin Fundraising," MSNBC, September 1, 2008, http://firstread.msnbc.msn.com/archive/2008/09/01/1320 772.aspx. Accessed July 23, 2009.
7. CBS News–*New York Times* poll, "A Woman President," February 5, 2006, http://www.cbsnews.com/htdocs/pdf/020306woman.pdf. Accessed July 11, 2009.
8. Interview with Thomas Riehle, Democratic pollster, March 22, 2009.
9. Joshua Green, "The Front-Runner's Fall," *The Atlantic,* September 2008.
10. Clinton campaign strategy memo from Mark Penn, as reprinted in the *Chicago Tribune*'s "The Swamp," Mark Silva, November 15, 2007.
11. Lester Holt, MSNBC, February 5, 2008, as reported by "Media Matters for America," February 6, 2008.
12. Jeffrey M. Jones, "Public Divided on Whether Obama Has Necessary Experience," Gallup, March 4, 2008.
13. Ibid.
14. Gary Langer, "EXIT POLL: Critical Clinton Wins," ABC News, March 4, 2008.
15. Hillary Clinton, as reported by *Newsweek,* January 7, 2008.
16. Hillary Clinton, Speech to Supporters, Washington, D.C., June 7, 2008.
17. Alaska governor Sarah Palin, Republican National Convention, September 3, 2008.
18. Ibid.
19. Joshua Green, "The Front-Runner's Fall," *The Atlantic,* September 2008.
20. Mike Allen, "Clinton Told to Portray Obama as Foreign," Politico.com, August 10, 2008, http://www.politico.com/news/stories/0808/12420.html. Accessed July 23, 2009.

21. Karen Tumulty, "The Five Mistakes Clinton Made," *Time,* May 8, 2008.
22. Katie Couric, "One-on-One with Sarah Palin," *CBS Evening News,* September 24, 2008, http://www.cbsnews.com/stories/2008/09/24/evening news/main4476173.shtml. Accessed July 11, 2009.
23. Mark Hugo Lopez, Emily Kirby, and Jared Sagoff, "Voter Turnout Among Young Women and Men," CIRCLE, January 2003, updated July 2005.
24. Ibid.
25. The Center for Information & Research on Civic Learning & Engagement, Electoral Engagement Among Non-College Attending Youth, http://www .civicyouth.org/PopUps/FactSheets/FS_04_noncollege_vote.pdf. Accessed July 23, 2009.
26. Mark Hugo Lopez, Emily Kirby, and Jared Sagoff, "Voter Turnout Among Young Women and Men," CIRCLE, January 2003, updated July 2005.
27. David Von Drehle, "Obama's Youth Vote Triumph," *Time,* January 4, 2008.
28. Ibid.
29. Kim Stolz, "Iowa '08: Obama's Victory Proves that Young People Aren't So Apathetic After All," MTV News, January 4, 2008.
30. George Washington University Graduate School of Political Management, "YOUNG VOTER MOBILIZATION TACTICS," 2006, http://www .civicyouth.org/PopUps/Young_Voters_Guide.pdf.
31. Andrew Romano, "He's One of Us Now," *Newsweek,* February 18, 2008.
32. Karlo Barrios Marcelo and Emily Hoban Kirby, "Quick Facts about U.S. Young Voters: The Presidential Election Year 2008," CIRCLE, October 2008.
33. CIRCLE, "Young Voters in the 2008 Presidential Election," November 24, 2008, http://www.civicyouth.org/PopUps/FactSheets/FS_08_exit_polls.pdf. Accessed July 23, 2009.
34. Gallup, "Election Polls—Vote by Groups, 2008," http://www.gallup.com/poll/112132/Election-Polls-Vote-Groups–2008.aspx.
35. CIRCLE, "Young Voters in the 2008 Presidential Election," November 24, 2008, http://www.civicyouth.org/PopUps/FactSheets/FS_08_exit_polls.pdf. Accessed July 23, 2009.
36. Ibid.
37. Gallup, "Election Polls—Vote by Groups, 2008," http://www.gallup.com/poll/112132/Election-Polls-Vote-Groups–2008.aspx. Accessed July 23, 2009.
38. Noam Cohen, "Don't Like Palin's Wikipedia Story? Change It," *New York Times,* August 31, 2008, http://www.nytimes.com/2008/09/01/technology/01link.html. Accessed July 23, 2009.
39. Camille Paglia, "Palin: Feminism's Greatest Leap Forward since Madonna," Salon.com, September 10, 2008.
40. Interview with Leslie Bradshaw, communications manager, New Media Strategies, March 8, 2008.
41. Report analysis provided by New Media Strategies, July 25, 2009.
42. David Hinckley, "Red-state Staple Rush Limbaugh's Radio Show Has a Loyal Audience in New York City," *New York Daily News,* March 12, 2009.

43. Pew Research Center for the People and the Press, "Online Papers Modestly Boost Newspaper Readership," July 30, 2006, http://people-press.org/report/282/online-papers-modestly-boost-newspaper-readership. Accessed July 23, 2009.

44. Nielsen Company, press release, "Social Networks & Blogs Now 4th Most Popular Online Activity, Ahead of Personal Email, Nielsen Reports," March 9, 2009, http://en-us.nielsen.com/main/news/news_releases/2009/march/social_networks_. Accessed July 23, 2009.

CHAPTER 5: FROM THE KITCHEN TO THE KITCHEN CABINET

1. All polls reported by Polling Report, http://www.pollingreport.com/politics.htm.

2. CBS News, "CBS Poll: Gender Matters More Than Race," March 19, 2008, http://www.cbsnews.com/stories/2008/03/19/opinion/polls/main3949396.shtml. Accessed July 23, 2009.

3. Lifetime Networks, "Every Woman Counts," December 3, 2008.

4. Nate Silver, "The Palin Paradox: Women More Likely to Be Elected in Male-Dominated Districts," June 7, 2009, http://www.fivethirtyeight.com/2009/06/palin-paradox-women-more-likely-to-be.html. Accessed July 11, 2009.

5. Andrew Kohut, "Are Americans Ready to Elect a Female President?," Pew Research Center for the People & the Press, May 9, 2007.

6. Andy Barr, "Palin Effect Not 'Long Lasting,'" Politico.com, October 7, 2008.

7. Debbie Walsh and Susan J. Carroll, "Gender Gap Evident in the 2008 Election: Women, Unlike Men, Show Clear Preference for Obama over McCain," Center for American Women in Politics, Rutgers University, November 5, 2008.

8. Women's Voices. Women Vote, press release, "Single Women Prove Decisive Political Force," November 5, 2008, http://www.wvwv.org/2008/11/5/single-women-prove-decisive-political-force. Accessed July 23, 2009.

9. CIRCLE, "Young Voters in the 2008 Presidential Election," November 24, 2008, http://www.civicyouth.org/PopUps/FactSheets/FS_08_exit_polls.pdf. Accessed July 23, 2009.

10. David Paul Kuhn, "Iowa voters reveal unexpected trends," Politico.com, January 4, 2008.

11. Richard Cohen, "'You're Likable Enough' Costs Obama," Real Clear Politics, January 10, 2008, http://www.realclearpolitics.com.

12. Rick Morin and Paul Taylor, "Revisiting the Mommy Wars," Pew Research Center, September 15, 2008.

13. Sharon Krum, "Why Women Really Should Rule," Guardian, March 26, 2008.

14. Vicky Haddock, "Are We Ready for a Woman President?" San Francisco Chronicle, April 27, 2007.

15. Caliper, "The Qualities That Distinguish Women Leaders," 2005, http://www.caliperonline.com/womenstudy/WomenLeaderWhitePaper.pdf. Accessed July 23, 2009.

16. Hilary Lips, "Women and Leadership: The Delicate Balancing Act," Radford University, http://www.womensmedia.com/new/Lips-Hilary-Women-as-Leaders.shtml. Accessed July 23, 2009.
17. Democratic Primary Debate, Manchester, New Hampshire, January 5, 2008.
18. Interview with Candy Crowley, CNN senior political correspondent, March 3, 2009.
19. Hilary Lips, "Women and Leadership: The Delicate Balancing Act," Radford University, http://www.womensmedia.com/new/Lips-Hilary-Women-as-Leaders.shtml. Accessed July 23, 2009.
20. Interview with Hilary Rosen, editor-at-large for the Huffington Post and CNN political contributor, March 28, 2009.
21. Jennifer Parker, "Michelle Obama Defends Patriotism, Jokes of 'Girl Fight' on 'View'," ABCnews.com, June 18, 2008, http://abcnews.go.com/Politics/Vote2008/story?id=5193627&page=1. Accessed July 23, 2009.
22. John M. Broder, "Biden Musings on Hillary Clinton," *New York Times,* September 10, 2008, http://thecaucus.blogs.nytimes.com/2008/09/10/biden-musings-on-hillary-clinton/. Accessed July 23, 2009.
23. Vicky Haddock, "Are We Ready for a Woman President?" *San Francisco Chronicle,* April 27, 2007.

CHAPTER 6: LADIES FIRST

1. Rachel L. Swarns, "First Lady in Control of Building Her Image," *New York Times,* April 25, 2009.
2. Maggie Jackson: "'First Mom' Has Other Role," *Boston Globe,* November 30, 2008.
3. Karen Travers and Yunji De Nies, "First Lady Crafts Role in White House," abcnews.go.com, March 4, 2009.
4. Frank Newport, "Michelle Obama's Speech Could Make a Difference," Gallup, August 25, 2008.
5. Jennifer Agiesta and Jon Cohen, "A Chance for the Candidates' Wives to Court Support," *Washington Post,* August 25, 2008.
6. Gallup, "Favorability: People in the News," from survey period September 5–7, 2008.
7. Patrick Healy, "New to Campaigning, but No Longer a Novice," *New York Times,* October 27, 2008.
8. Anne E. Kornblut, "For Bill Clinton, Echoes of Jackson in Obama Win," *Washington Post,* January 26, 2008, http://voices.washingtonpost.com/44/2008/01/26/for_bill_clinton_echoes_of_jac.html. Accessed July 11, 2009.
9. Remarks by Michelle Obama, Milwaukee, Wisconsin, February 18, 2008 [widely reported].
10. Foxnews.com, "Michelle Obama Takes Heat for Saying She's 'Proud of My Country' for the First Time," February 19, 2008.
11. Obama campaign spokesman Bill Burton, as reported by ABC News' Jack Tapper, February 18, 2008.

12. Michelle Obama, speech, Milwaukee, Wisconsin, February 18, 2008. http://blogs.abcnews.com/politicalpunch/2008/02/michelle-obam–1.html. Accessed June 12, 2009.
13. Andy Sullivan, "Laura Bush Defends Michelle Obama," Reuters Blogs, June 9, 2008.
14. Darren K. Carlson, "Ideal First Lady: Hillary Clinton or Laura Bush," Gallup, July 13, 2004.
15. Ibid.
16. Jeffrey M. Jones, "Laura Bush Leaves White House as Popular Figure," Gallup, January 14, 2009.
17. Ibid.
18. Gallup, "Favorability: People in the News," [over time], http://www.gallup.com/poll/1618/Favorability-People-News.aspx#1.
19. Patrick Healy, "New to Campaigning, but No Longer a Novice," *New York Times,* October 27, 2008.
20. Ibid.
21. Jennifer Parker, "Michelle Obama Defends Patriotism, Jokes of 'Girl Fight' on 'View'," ABCnews.com, June 18, 2008, http://abcnews.go.com/Politics/Vote2008/story?id=5193627&page=1.
22. First Lady Michelle Obama, Remarks to Employees of the Department of Housing and Urban Development, as quoted by Ed O'Keefe, "Michelle Obama Visits HUD," *Washington Post,* February 4, 2009.
23. Interview with Hilary Rosen, editor-at-large for the Huffington Post and CNN political contributor, March 28, 2009.
24. Maureen Dowd, "Should Michelle Cover Up?" *New York Times,* March 7, 2009.
25. Lifetime Networks, "Every Woman Counts," December 3, 2008.

CHAPTER 7: WHAT'S NEXT

1. Quentin Letts, "Oh Yes, Minister! Meet the women voted the world's most stunning politicians (what WOULD Sir Humphrey say . . .)," March 26, 2009, http://www.dailymail.co.uk/femail/article–1164890/Oh-Yes-Minister-Meet-women-voted-worlds-stunning-politicians-WOULD-Sir-Humphrey-say—.html. Accessed July 23, 2009.
2. Lifetime Networks, "Every Woman Counts," December 3, 2008.
3. Kate Zernike, "She Just Might Be President Someday," *New York Times,* May 18, 2008.
4. Roger Simon, "Is Sarah Palin Preparing for 2012?" Politico.com, October 28, 2008.
5. Matt Littman, "Sarah Palin in 2012? Get Ready For It," Huffington Post, October 8, 2008.
6. Michael Maiello, "Palin in 2012?," Forbes.com, October 28, 2008, http://blogs.forbes.com/trailwatch/2008/10/palin-in–2012.html. Accessed July 22, 2009.
7. Scott Conroy, "Palin Reveals 2012 Plans: Kindergarten for Son," November 5, 2008, http://www.cbsnews.com/blogs/2008/11/05/politics/fromtheroad/entry4576840.shtml. Accessed July 11, 2009.

8. Sam Stein, "SarahPAC: Palin Launches Political Action Committee, Prep for 2012," January 27, 2009, http://www.huffingtonpost.com/2009/01/27/sarahpac-palin-sets-up-po_n_161293.html. Accessed July 11, 2009.

9. Jon Cohen and Philip Rucker, "Palin Favorability Rating Dips As She Nears Exit, Poll Finds," *Washington Post,* July 24, 2009. Available at http://www.washingtonpost.com/wp-dyn/content/article/2009/07/23/AR2009072303799.html. Accessed July 27, 2009.

10. Reihan Salam, "The GOP in 2012," *The Atlantic,* March 10, 2009.

11. Gallup, "Clinton Starts Hearings with Strong Public Image," January 13, 2009.

12. Lifetime Networks, "Every Woman Counts," December 3, 2008.

13. Keren Blankfeld Schultz, "Billionaire Women We Admire," *Forbes,* March 11, 2009.

14. "Meg Whitman for Governor," http://www.megwhitman.com/platform.php. Accessed July 23, 2009.

15. Ibid.

16. Vicki Haddock, "Are We Ready for a Woman President?," *San Francisco Chronicle,* April 27, 2007.

17. UrbanDictionary.com, http://www.urbandictionary.com/define.php?term=chola. Accessed July 11, 2009.

CHAPTER 8: WHAT DO WOMEN DO N.O.W.?

1. Jo Freeman, "Political Organization in the Feminist Movement," 1974, http://uic.edu/orgs/cwluherstory/jofreeman/socialmovements/polorg.htm. Accessed June 11, 2009.

2. Interview with Andrew Rasiej, the founder of Personal Democracy Forum, May 1, 2009.

3. NPR, "Obama Supporters Rap Their Candidate on FISA," July 9, 2008, http://www.npr.org/templates/story/story.php?storyId=92357038. Accessed July 23, 2009.

4. Glenn Greenwald, "Obama's New Statement on FISA," July 3, 2008, http://utdocuments.blogspot.com/2008/07/obamas-new-statement-on-fisa.html. Accessed June 12, 2009.

5. Interview with Teri Christoph, Smart Girl Politics, June 14, 2009.

6. Interview with Liza Sabato, founder and lead blogger at Culture Kitchen.com, June 11, 2009.

7. "Girl fight," YouTube, posted February 2006: http://www.youtube.com/watch?v=E4Vh0i5lUw8. The video has had nearly 2.5 million views. Accessed July 27, 2009.

8. Sarah Palin, "The 'Cap and Tax' Dead End," *Washington Post,* July 14, 2009.

9. Girl Scout Research Institute, "The New Leadership Landscape: What Girls Say about Election 2008," January 13, 2009, http://www.girlscouts.org/news/news_releases/2009/leadership_landscape_2008_summary.pdf. Accessed July 23, 2009.

10. Ibid.

INDEX